D0010273

Falling into life

essays by
Leonard Kriegel

North Point Press
San Francisco *1991*

Printed in the United States of America

Library of Congress
Cataloging-in-Publication Data
Kriegel, Leonard, 1933–
Falling into life : essays / by Leonard Kriegel.
p. cm.
ISBN 0-86547-458-3
I. Title.
PS3561.R55F3 1991
814′.54—dc20 90-47346

Like the first one,
this one is for Harriet

Contents

Acknowledgments

I have made a number of changes in the essays that follow since their original publication in *The American Scholar*, *Confrontation*, *The Georgia Review*, *The Gettysburg Review*, *The Nation*, *The New York Times Magazine*, *Partisan Review*, *Present Tense*, *The Raritan Review*, *The Sewanee Review*, and *Social Policy*.

A writer's debts are usually too numerous to mention. It may be that they are best left unnamed, since the writer alone is ultimately responsible for what he says. But I would like to acknowledge a number of editors of those "small" magazines which remain at the heart of literary culture. In their politics, their cultural loyalties, and their relationship to this country and its writers, they are a remarkably diverse group. Perhaps the only things they truly share are a passion for the sentence and a conviction—despite all evidence to the contrary—that writing matters. The essays that follow weren't originally conceived in that way, but I like to think of them as a tip of the hat to editors—in particular to George Core, Joseph Epstein, Stan Lindberg, Elizabeth Pochoda, Richard Poirier, Murray Polner, William Phillips, and Peter Stitt. To each of them goes one writer's thank-you, and an additional thank-you to another writer, Ross Feld, who as friend and editor helped put this book in shape.

Introduction

A few months ago, while rummaging through a cardboard box containing old photographs and postcards, I discovered a letter I had written from Paris to my wife in May of 1965. I was immediately struck by the painful intimacy with which I had confessed need and fear to a woman I love enough to trust. Although the essays in this book are very personal, I have long since learned that intimacy alone does not guarantee coherence. Rereading that letter brings memory enough, and I have no desire to quote from it here.

But I can think of no better way to preface what follows than by reconstructing the circumstances under which that letter was written. Since August, Harriet and I had been living in Holland with our two-year-old son. For nine months we had lived a life as close to idyllic as anything I had ever known. We lived in a still-quaint Dutch coastal village, the windows of our apartment overlooking the turbulence of the North Sea. I was serving as the Fulbright lecturer in American literature at the University of Leiden that year. Two days earlier, I had left my wife and son in Noordwijk Aan Zee while I went to Paris, where I was to deliver a talk on John Steinbeck. From Paris I was to fly to London. In all, I would be away from wife and child for ten days.

This was my first time in Paris alone. And more than any other city I know, Paris should be shared with friend or lover. Shared, it endows one's existence with the shape of its contours. But to be alone in Paris is to find oneself more isolated than in any other city.

I felt both lonely and isolated in Paris that day. And as I propelled myself on my braces and crutches from the hotel near the place Vendôme where I was staying to the cafe near Saint-Germain des Prés, close to where I was to deliver my lecture later that afternoon, I grew irritated with the loneliness that gripped me. On the swing-through gait of an experienced crutch-walker, I hurled myself through the streets and avenues of this most graceful of all great cities. Never before had I felt so distant from its charm and majesty. And when I sat down in the cafe to shelter myself from the brisk May wind that sent clouds spinning across the rooftops of Paris, I still felt lonely and isolated. Paris itself seemed raw, brittle, uncharacteristically frayed. I had walked four or five miles, but the city's beauty simply offended me.

Two weeks earlier I had walked through these same streets with my wife and my son. I missed them now. I ordered a glass of wine and pulled from my inside jacket pocket the stationery I had taken from my hotel. As I began to write to Harriet, my eyes caught the glint of sun flagging the aluminum crutches I had reflexively hung on the back of the wooden chair next to where I was sitting. I took a sip of the wine the waiter brought and tried to focus once again on my letter to my wife. And then I suddenly gasped, stifling a sob as if I had been hit in the solar plexus and could feel myself doubling over. The reality I had lived with for twenty-one years had once again overwhelmed me. *I was a cripple.* And I missed the legs I had lost to a polio virus far more than I missed the wife and son I loved. The loss of my legs enraged me. It would always enrage me. And I would never get used to it. Its arbitrariness, its naked proclamation of what I could and could not do, of what I could never again do, its failure to allow me compensation for what had been so brusquely taken—I had lived with such intimate knowledge of incapacity for more than two decades. And I would be forced to live with that knowledge for whatever time remained to me here on earth. Even this clutching rage was testimony to the triumph of the virus.

Overwhelmed by rage and loss, I forced myself, as three days earlier I had forced myself to burrow into the wind coming off the sea in Noordwijk, to write that letter to my wife. I was doing what hundreds of other American writers in hundreds of other Paris cafes had done. Only I wasn't like those others. *I was a cripple.* That fact had defined me for twenty-one years. And it would continue to define me—as man, as husband, as father, as teacher; above all, as writer.

That was not the first time love and loss melded in my life. But it was a moment when my accomplishments and my broken aspirations, framed by the swell of rage and loss, locked into a clarity so precise that all the contradictions with which I had been living since I took sick were set before me. To be both a cripple and a writer forced a confrontation with the boundaries of rage and loss even as they intersected with the boundaries of pride.

Once again I had been transformed by rage, the rage of a writer forced to acknowledge that his fate has been determined by an accidental encounter with a virus. I had been transformed by rage before, but this time it burned so hard and clear that I felt the rules of survival etch themselves into my brain. It was not the absence of "normal" legs that fueled my overwhelming sense of anger and loss. My loss was more than physical. And it was certainly not that I had failed to meet the challenge of the polio virus that struck me down when I was eleven. The vanity of a man who has "overcome a handicap" is formidable. I had earned my survival. And I knew it.

But the rage created by loss is more formidable still. And it is that rage that lies behind each of the essays in this book. Whether they are analytical or depict the cripple's condition as a paradigm for the state of modern man or simply reconstruct the way loss felt, these essays have in common an unstifled rage, a rage born of absence and framed by longing. Shakespeare's crippled king, Richard III, speaks of it when he offers himself as "unfinished" and "rudely stamped." I, too, am rudely stamped. Over and over again, I thrust myself against a writer's memory and an eleven-year-old boy's ambition. The one guards my sense of the way life was; the other grinds me against possibilities never realized, the things I could never do growing greater and greater as they are ransomed by my imagination. And if these essays speak truthfully of loss, then they must speak of the loss not merely of legs but of all those possibilities that might have been.

I offer them aware that there is something a bit ludicrous about the desires I still feel. But the fact is that I still feel them. A man in his mid-fifties should no longer trail the clouds of glory of an adolescence that never came. In the solidity of middle age, I should be sufficiently used to never again being able to box, to run on the beach, to hike, to dance, to play ball, to make love with the thrust of legs. By now I should be inoculated against loss as children are today inoculated against the virus that took my legs.

But these essays about being crippled testify to a different point of view. I have yet to gain the philosophical detachment that comes with age. Perhaps more to the point, I no longer want to achieve that detachment. A man can meet himself even on his way down. And these essays, written over the past decade, were for me a way of meeting myself. Language contains loss and language certifies absence. Better still, language preserves love. Even as fragments of a life, there is a record here. If it is a record that speaks of the absence and rage that seized me as I sat in that cafe in Paris writing a letter to my wife some twenty-five years ago, I hope that it is also a record that speaks of the peculiar gratitude that sometimes accompanies loss. Rage is the immediate gift of that loss. But if you are lucky, love and pride follow.

I am still angry about the loss of my legs. I suspect I shall be angry when I draw my dying breath. Yet these essays also speak of my pride in my performance. All things considered, I have done well. I managed, after all, to push my brace-bound body through those miles of Paris streets on that May afternoon. Nature might have been my enemy, but a writer's imagination could teach even a cripple how to ignore the restrictions imposed by nature. I didn't need Shakespeare's Richard to teach me that. It came with the territory.

Three weeks earlier, when my family and I were vacationing in Paris, I had walked through the Tuileries with Harriet on my left and my son grasping the pinky thrust out from the crutch I held in my right hand. Benji walked as proudly as any other two-year-old moving along with his father. For my son, this was "normal" enough, the way we had always walked together, a surety of trust and touch binding us. We were heading for the puppeteers of the Grand Guignol. And as we walked, I felt not the rage born of loss but the vanity born of pride. I had earned this trusting grip of my son's hand on my pinky. For I had made the only bargain with fate a cripple and a writer could make. I had survived. And I would preserve that survival in the language of record. I hope that in the essays that follow the joy of that survival is as apparent as the rage. As a writer, I cherish them both. As a man, I have made my peace with neither.

Falling
into
life

Falling into life

It is not the actual death a man is doomed to die but the deaths his imagination anticipates that claim attention as he grows older. We are constantly being reminded that the prospect of death forcefully concentrates the mind. While that may be so, it is not a prospect that does very much else for the imagination—other than to make us aware of its limitations and imbalances.

Over the past five years, as I have moved into the solidity of middle age, my own most formidable imaginative limitation has turned out to be a surprising need for symmetry. I am possessed by a peculiar passion: I want to believe that my life has been balanced out. And because I once had to learn to fall in order to keep that life mine, I now seem to have convinced myself that I must also learn to fall into death.

Falling into life wasn't easy, and I suspect that is why I hunger for such awkward symmetry today. Having lost the use of my legs during the polio epidemic that swept across the eastern United States during the summer of 1944, I was soon immersed in a process of rehabilitation that was, at least when looked at in retrospect, as much spiritual as physical.

That was a full decade before the discovery of the Salk vaccine ended polio's reign as the disease most dreaded by America's parents and their children. Treatment of the disease had been standardized by 1944: following the initial onslaught of the virus, patients were kept in isolation for a period of ten days to two weeks. Following that, orthodox medical opinion was content to subject patients to as much heat as they could stand. Stiff, paralyzed limbs were swathed in heated, coarse woolen towels known as "hot packs." (The towels were the same greenish brown as the blankets issued to American GIs, and they reinforced a boy's sense of being at war.) As soon as the hot packs had baked enough pain and stiffness out of a patient's body that he could be moved on and off a stretcher, the treatment was ended, and the patient faced a series of daily immersions in a heated pool.

I was ultimately to spend two full years at the appropriately named New York State Reconstruction Home in West Haverstraw. But what I remember most vividly about my stay there was, in the first three months, being submerged in a hot pool six times a day for periods of between fifteen and twenty minutes. I would lie on a stainless steel slab, only my face out of the water, while the wet heat rolled against my dead legs and the physical therapist at my side worked at a series of manipulations intended to bring my useless muscles back to health.

Each immersion was a baptism by fire in the water. While my mind pitched and reeled with memories of the "normal" boy I had been a few weeks earlier, I would close my eyes and focus not, as my therapist urged, on bringing dead legs back to life but on my strange fall from the childhood grace of the physical. Like all eleven-year-old boys, I had a spent a good deal of time thinking about my body. Before the attack of the virus, however, I thought about it only in connection with my own lunge toward adolescence. Never before had my body seemed an object in itself. Now it was. And like the twenty-one other boys in the ward—all of us between the ages of nine and twelve—I sensed I would never move beyond that fall from grace, even as I played with memories of the way I once had been.

Each time I was removed from the hot water and placed on a stretcher by the side of the pool, there to await the next immersion, I was fed salt tablets. These were simply intended to make up for the sweat we lost, but salt tablets seemed to me the cruelest confirmation of my new status as spiritual debtor. Even today, more than four decades later, I still shiver at the mere thought of those salt tablets. Sometimes the hospital orderly would literally have to pry my mouth open to force me to swallow them. I dreaded the nausea the taste of salt inspired in me. Each time I was resubmerged in the hot pool, I would grit my teeth—not from the flush of heat sweeping over my body but from the thought of what I would have to face when I would again be taken out of the water. To be an eater of salt was far more humiliating than to endure pain. Nor was I alone in feeling this way. After lights-out had quieted the ward, we boys would furtively whisper from cubicle to cubicle of how we dreaded being forced to swallow salt tablets. It was that, rather than the pain we endured, that anchored our sense of loss and dread.

Any recovery of muscle use in a polio patient usually took place within three months of the disease's onset. We all knew that. But as time passed, every boy in the ward learned to recite stories of those who, like Lazarus, had witnessed their own bodily resurrection. Having fallen from physical grace, we also chose to fall away from the reality in front of us. Our therapists were skilled and dedicated, but they weren't wonder-working saints. Paralyzed legs and arms rarely responded to their manipulations.

We could not admit to ourselves, or to them, that we were permanently crippled. But each of us knew without knowing that his future was tied to the body that floated on the stainless steel slab.

We sweated out the hot pool and we choked on the salt tablets, and through it all we looked forward to the promise of rehabilitation. For, once the stiffness and pain had been baked and boiled out of us, we would no longer be eaters of salt. We would not be what we once had been, but at least we would be candidates for reentry into the world, admittedly made over to face its demands encased in leather and steel.

I suppose we might have been told that our fall from grace was permanent. But I am still grateful that no one—neither doctors nor nurses nor therapists, not even that sadistic orderly, himself a former polio patient, who limped through our lives and through our pain like some vengeful presence—told me that my chances of regaining the use of my legs were nonexistent. Like every other boy in the ward, I organized my needs around whatever illusions were available. And the illusion I needed above any other was that one morning I would simply wake up and rediscover the "normal" boy of memory, once again playing baseball in French Charley's Field in Bronx Park rather than roaming the fields of his own imagination. At the age of eleven, I needed to weather reality, not face it. And to this very day I silently thank those who were concerned enough about me, or indifferent enough to my fate, not to tell me what they knew.

Like most boys, sick or well, I was an adaptable creature—and rehabilitation demanded adaptability. The fall from bodily grace transformed each of us into an acolyte of the possible, a pragmatic American for whom survival was method and strategy. We would learn, during our days in the New York State Reconstruction Home, to confront the world that was. We would learn to survive the way we were, with whatever the virus had left intact.

7 Falling into life

I had fallen away from the body's prowess, but I was being led toward a life measured by different standards. Even as I fantasized about the past, it disappeared. Rehabilitation, I was to learn, was ahistorical, a future devoid of any significant claim on the past. Rehabilitation was a thief's primer of compensation and deception: its purpose was to teach one how to steal a touch of the normal from an existence that would be striking in its abnormality.

When I think back to those two years in the ward, the boy who made his rehabilitation most memorable was Joey Tomashevski. Joey was the son of an upstate dairy farmer, a Polish immigrant who had come to America before the Depression and whose English was even poorer than the English of my own *shtetl*-bred father. The virus had left both of Joey's arms so lifeless and atrophied that with pinky and thumb I could circle where his bicep should have been and still stick the forefinger of my other hand through. And yet Joey assumed that he would make do with whatever had been left him. He accepted without question the task of making his toes and feet into fingers and hands. With lifeless arms encased in a canvas sling that looked like the breadbasket a European peasant might carry to market, Joey would sit up in bed and demonstrate how he could maneuver fork and spoon with his toes.

I would never have dreamed of placing such confidence in my fingers, let alone my toes. I found, as most of the other boys in the ward did, Joey's unabashed pride in the flexibility and control with which he could maneuver a forkful of mashed potatoes into his mouth a continuous indictment of my sense of the world's natural order. We boys with dead legs would gather round his bed in our wheelchairs and silently watch Joey display his dexterity with a vanity so open and naked that it seemed an invitation to being struck down yet again. But Joey's was a vanity already tested by experience. For he was more than willing to accept whatever challenges the virus threw his way. For the sake of demonstrating his skill to us, he kicked a basketball from the auditorium stage through the hoop attached to a balcony some fifty feet away. When one of our number derisively called him "lucky," he proceeded to kick five of seven more balls through that same hoop.

I suspect that Joey's pride in his ability to compensate for what had been taken away from him irritated me because I knew that, before I could pursue my own rehabilitation with such singular passion, I had to surrender myself to what was being demanded of me. And that meant I had to learn to fall. It meant that I had to learn, as Joey Tomashevski had already learned, how to transform absence into opportunity. Even though I still lacked Joey's instinctive willingness to live with the legacy of the virus, I found myself being overhauled, re-created in much the same way as a car engine is rebuilt. Nine months after I arrived in the ward, a few weeks before my twelfth birthday, I was fitted for double long-legged braces bound together by a steel pelvic band circling my waist. Lifeless or not, my legs were precisely measured, the steel carefully molded to form, screws and locks and leather joined to one another for my customized benefit. It was technology that would hold me up—another offering on the altar of compensation. "You get what you give," said Jackie Lyons, my closest friend in the ward. For he, too, was now a novitiate of the possible. He, too, now had to learn how to choose the road back.

Falling into life was not a metaphor; it was real, a process learned only through doing, the way a baby learns to crawl, to stand, and then to walk. After the steel bands around calves and thighs and pelvis had been covered over by the rich-smelling leather, after the braces had been precisely fitted to allow my fear-ridden imagination the surety of their holding presence, I was pulled to my feet. For the first time in ten months, I stood. Two middle-aged craftsmen, the hospital bracemakers who worked in a machine shop deep in the basement, held me in place as my therapist wedged two wooden crutches beneath my shoulders.

They stepped back, first making certain that my grip on the crutches was firm. Filled with pride in their technological prowess, the three of them stood in front of me, admiring their skill. Had I been created in the laboratory of Mary Shelley's Dr. Frankenstein, I could not have felt myself any more the creature of scientific pride. I stood on the braces, crutches beneath my shoulders slanting outward like twin towers of Pisa. I flushed, swallowed hard, struggled to keep from crying, struggled not to be overwhelmed by my fear of falling.

My future had arrived. The leather had been fitted, the screws had been turned to the precise millimeter, the locks at the knees and the bushings at the ankles had been properly tested and retested. That very afternoon I was taken for the first time to a cavernous room filled with barbells and Indian clubs and crutches and walkers. I would spend an hour each day there for the next six months. In the rehab room I would learn how to mount two large wooden steps made to the exact measure of a New York City bus's. I would swing on parallel bars from one side to the other, my arms learning how they would have to hurl me through the world. I balanced Indian clubs like a circus juggler because my therapist insisted it would help my coordination. And I was expected to learn to fall.

I was a dutiful patient. I did as I was told, because I could see no advantage to doing anything else. I hungered for the approval of those in authority—doctors, nurses, therapists, the two bracemakers. Again and again, my therapist demonstrated how I was to throw my legs from the hip. Again and again, I did as I was told. Grabbing the banister with my left hand, I threw my leg from the hip while pushing off my right crutch. Like some baby elephant (despite the sweat lost in the heated pool, the months of inactivity in bed had fattened me up considerably), I dangled from side to side on the parallel bars. Grunting with effort, I did everything demanded of me. I did it with an unabashed eagerness to please those who had power over my life. I wanted to put myself at risk. I wanted to do whatever was supposed to be "good" for me. I believed as absolutely as I have ever believed in anything that rehabilitation would finally placate the hunger of the virus.

But when my therapist commanded me to fall, I cringed. The prospect of falling terrified me. Every afternoon, as I worked through my prescribed activities, I prayed that I would be able to fall when the session ended. Falling was the most essential "good" of all the "goods" held out for my consideration by my therapist. I believed that. I believed it so intensely that the belief itself was painful. Everything else asked of me was given, and given gladly. I mounted the bus stairs, pushed across the parallel bars until my arms ached with the effort, allowed the medicine ball to pummel me, flailed away at the empty air with my fists because my therapist wanted me to rid myself of the tension within. The slightest sign of approval from those in authority was enough to make me puff with pleasure. Other boys in the ward might not have taken rehabilitation seriously, but I was an eager servant cringing before the promise of approval.

Only I couldn't fall. As each session ended, I would be led to the mats that took up a full third of the huge room. "It's time," the therapist would say. Dutifully, I would follow her, step after step. Just as dutifully, I would stand on the edge of those two-inch-thick mats, staring down at them until I could feel my body quiver. "All you have to do is let go," my therapist assured me. "The other boys do it. Just let go and fall."

But the prospect of letting go was precisely what terrified me.

That the other boys in the ward had no trouble in falling added to my shame and terror. I didn't need my therapist to tell me the two-inch-thick mats would keep me from hurting myself. I knew there was virtually no chance of injury when I fell, but that knowledge simply made me more ashamed of a cowardice that was as monumental as it was unexplainable. Had it been able to rid me of my sense of my own cowardice, I would happily have settled for bodily harm. But I was being asked to surrender myself to the emptiness of space, to let go and crash down to the mats below, to feel myself suspended in air when nothing stood between me and the vacuum of the world. *That* was the prospect that overwhelmed me. *That* was what left me sweating with rage and humiliation. The contempt I felt was for my own weakness.

I tried to justify what I sensed could never be justified. Why should I be expected to throw myself into emptiness? Was this sullen terror the price of compensation, the badge of normality? Maybe my refusal to fall embodied some deeper thrust than I could then understand. Maybe I had unconsciously seized upon some fundamental resistance to the forces that threatened to overwhelm me. What did it matter that the ground was covered with the thick mats? The tremors I feared were in my heart and soul.

Shame plagued me—and shame is the older brother to disease. Flushing with shame, I would stare down at the mats. I could feel myself wanting to cry out. But I shriveled at the thought of calling more attention to my cowardice. I would finally hear myself whimper, "I'm sorry. But I can't. I can't let go."

Formless emptiness. A rush of air through which I would plummet toward obliteration. As my "normal" past grew more and more distant, I reached for it more and more desperately, recalling it like some movie whose plot has long since been forgotten but whose scenes continue to comfort through images disconnected from anything but themselves. I remembered that there had been a time when the prospect of falling evoked not terror but joy: football games on the rain-softened autumn turf of Mosholu Parkway, belly-flopping on an American Flyer down its snow-covered slopes in winter, rolling with a pack of friends down one of the steep hills in Bronx Park. Free-falls from the past, testifying not to a loss of the self but to an absence of barriers.

My therapist pleaded, ridiculed, cajoled, threatened, bullied. I was sighed over and railed at. But I couldn't let go and fall. I couldn't sell my terror off so cheaply. Ashamed as I was, I wouldn't allow myself to be bullied out of terror.

A month passed—a month of struggle between me and my therapist. Daily excursions to the rehab room, daily practice runs through the future that was awaiting me. The daily humiliation of discovering that one's own fear had been transformed into a public issue, a subject of discussion among the other boys in the ward, seemed unending.

And then terror simply evaporated. It was as if I had served enough time in that prison. I was ready to move on. One Tuesday afternoon, as my session ended, the therapist walked resignedly alongside me toward the mats. "All right, Leonard. It's time again. All you have to do is let go and fall." Again I stood above the mats. Only this time it was as if something beyond my control or understanding had decided to let my body's fall from grace take me down for good. I was not seized by the usual paroxysm of fear. I didn't feel myself break out in a terrified sweat. It was over.

I don't mean that I suddenly felt myself spring into courage. That wasn't what happened at all. The truth was I had simply been worn down into letting go, like a boxer in whose eyes one recognizes not the flicker of defeat—that issue never having been in doubt—but the acceptance of defeat. Letting go no longer held my imagination captive. I found myself quite suddenly faced with a necessary fall—a fall into life.

So it was that I stood above the mat and heard myself sigh and then felt myself let go, dropping through the quiet air, crutches slipping off to the sides. What I didn't feel this time was the threat of my body slipping into emptiness, so mummified by the terror before it that the touch of air preempted even death. I dropped. I did not crash. I dropped. I did not collapse. I dropped. I did not plummet. I felt myself enveloped by a curiously gentle moment in my life. In that sliver of time before I hit the mat, I was kissed by space.

My body absorbed the slight shock and I rolled onto my back, braced legs swinging like unguided missiles into the free air, crutches dropping away to the sides. Even as I fell through the air, I could sense the shame and fear drain from my soul, and I knew that my sense of my own cowardice would soon follow. In falling, I had given myself a new start, a new life.

"That's it!" my therapist shouted triumphantly. "You let go! And there it is!"

You let go! And there it is! Yes, and you discover not terror but the only self you are going to be allowed to claim anyhow. You fall free, and then you learn that those padded mats hold not courage but the unclaimed self. And if it turned out to be not the most difficult of tasks, did that make my sense of jubilation any less?

From that moment, I gloried in my ability to fall. Falling became an end in itself. I lost sight of what my therapist had desperately been trying to demonstrate for me—that there was a purpose in learning how to fall. She wanted to teach me through the fall what I would have to face in the future. She wanted to give me a wholeness I could not give myself. For she knew that mine would be a future so different from what confronts the "normal" that I had to learn to fall into life in order not to be overwhelmed.

From that day, she urged me to practice falling as if I were a religious disciple being urged by a master to practice spiritual discipline. Letting go meant allowing my body to float into space, to turn at the direction of the fall and follow the urgings of emptiness. For her, learning to fall was learning that most essential of American lessons: How to turn incapacity into capacity.

"You were afraid of hurting yourself," she explained to me. "But that's the beauty of it. When you let go, you can't hurt yourself."

An echo of the streets and playgrounds I called home until I met the virus. American slogans: Go with the flow, roll with the punch, slide with the threat until it is no longer a threat. They were simple slogans, and they were all intended to create strength from weakness, a veritable world's fair of compensation.

I returned to the city a year later. By that time I was a willing convert, one who now secretly enjoyed demonstrating his ability to fall. I enjoyed the surprise that would greet me as I got to my feet, unscathed. However perverse it may seem, I felt a certain pleasure when, as I walked with a friend, I felt a crutch slip out of my grasp. Watching the thrust of concern darken his features, I felt myself in control of my own capacity. For falling had become the way my body sought out its proper home. It was an earthbound body, and mine would be an earthbound life. My quest would be for the solid ground beneath me. Falling with confidence, I fell away from terror and fear.

Of course, some falls took me unawares, and I found myself letting go too late or too early. Bruised in ego and sometimes in body, I would pull myself to my feet to consider what had gone wrong. Yet I was essentially untroubled. Such defeats were part of the game, even when they confined me to bed for a day or two afterward. I was an accountant of pain, and sometimes heavier payment was demanded. In my mid-thirties, I walked my two-year-old son's babysitter home, tripped on the curbstone, and broke my wrist. At forty-eight, an awkward fall triggered by a carelessly unlocked brace sent me smashing against the bathtub and into surgery for a broken femur. It took four months for me to learn to walk with the crutches all over again. But I learned. I already knew how to fall.

I knew such accidents could be handled. After all, pain was not synonymous with mortality. In fact, pain was insurance against an excessive consciousness of mortality. Pain might validate the specific moment in time, but it didn't have much to do with the future. I did not yet believe that falling into life had anything to do with falling into death. It was simply a way for me to exercise control over my own existence.

It seems to me today that when I first let my body fall to those mats, I was somehow giving myself the endurance I would need to survive in this world. In a curious way, falling became a way of celebrating what I had lost. My legs were lifeless, useless, but their loss had created a dancing image in whose shadowy gyrations I recognized a strange but potentially interesting new self. I would survive. I knew that now. I could let go, I could fall, and, best of all, I could get up.

To create an independent self, a man had to rid himself both of the myths that nurtured him and the myths that held him back. Learning to fall had been the first lesson in how I yet might live successfully as a cripple. Even disease had its inviolate principles. I understood that the most dangerous threat to the sense of self I needed was an inflated belief in my own capacity. Falling rid a man of excess baggage; it taught him how each of us is dependent on balance.

But what really gave falling legitimacy was the knowledge that I could get to my feet again. That was what made letting go a fall into life. That was what taught me the rules of survival. As long as I could pick myself up and stand on my own two feet, brace-bound and crutch-propped as I was, the fall testified to my ability to live in the here and now, to stake my claim as an American who had turned incapacity into capacity. For such a man, falling might well be considered the language of everyday achievement.

But the day came, as I knew it must come, when I could no longer pick myself up. It was then that my passion for symmetry in endings began. On that day, spurred on by another fall, I found myself spinning into the inevitable future.

The day was actually a rainy night in November of 1983. I had just finished teaching at the City College Center for Worker Education, an off-campus degree program for working adults, and had joined some friends for dinner. All of us, I remember, were in a jovial, celebratory mood, although I no longer remember what it was we were celebrating. Perhaps it was simply the satisfaction of being good friends and colleagues at dinner together.

We ate in a Spanish restaurant on 14th Street in Manhattan. It was a dinner that took on, for me at least, the intensity of a time that would assume greater and greater significance as I grew older, one of those watershed moments writers are so fond of. In the dark, rainswept New York night, change and possibility seemed to drift like a thick fog all around us.

Our mood was still convivial when we left the restaurant around eleven o'clock. The rain had slackened off to a soft drizzle and the streetlights glistened on the wet black creosote. At night, rain in the city has a way of transforming proportion into optimism. The five of us stood around on the slicked-down sidewalk, none of us willing to be the first to break the richness of the mood by leaving.

17 Falling into life

Suddenly the crutch in my left hand began to slip out from under me, slowly, almost deliberately, as if the crutch had a mind of its own and had not yet made the commitment that would send me down. I had apparently hit a slick patch of city sidewalk, some nub of concrete worn smooth as medieval stone by thousands of shoppers and panhandlers and tourists and students who daily pounded the bargain hustlings of 14th Street.

Instinctively, I at first tried to fight the fall, to seek for balance by pushing off from the crutch in my right hand. But as I recognized that the fall was inevitable, I simply went slack—and for the thousandth time my body sought vindication in its ability to let go and drop. These good friends had seen me fall before. They knew my childish vanities, understood that I still thought of falling as a way to demonstrate my control of the traps and uncertainties that lay in wait for us all.

Thirty-eight years earlier, I had discovered that I could fall into life simply by letting go. Now I made a different discovery—that I could no longer get to my feet by myself. I hit the wet ground and quickly turned over and pushed up, trying to use one of the crutches as a prop to boost myself to my feet, as I had been taught to do as a boy of twelve.

But try as hard as I could, I couldn't get to my feet. It wasn't that I lacked physical strength. I knew that my arms were as powerful as ever as I pushed down on the wet concrete. It had nothing to do with the fact that the street was wet, as my friends insisted later. No, it had to do with a subtle, mysterious change in my own sense of rhythm and balance. My body had decided—*and decided on its own, autonomously*—that the moment had come for me to face the question of endings. It was the body that chose its time of recognition.

It was, it seems to me now, a distinctively American moment. It left me pondering limitations and endings and summations. It left me with the curiously buoyant sense that mortality had quite suddenly made itself a felt presence rather than the rhetorical strategy used by the poets and novelists I taught to my students. This was what writers had in mind when they spoke of the truly common fate, this sense of ending coming to one unbidden. This had brought with it my impassioned quest for symmetry. As I lay on the wet ground—no more than a minute or two—all I could think of was how much I wanted my life to balance out. It was as if I were staring into a future in which time itself had evaporated.

Here was a clear, simple perception, and there was nothing mystical about it. There are limitations we recognize and those that recognize us. My friends, who had been standing around nervously while I tried to get to my feet, finally asked if they could help me up. "You'll have to," I said. "I can't get up any other way."

Two of them pulled me to my feet while another jammed the crutches beneath my arms, as the therapist and the two bracemakers had done almost four decades earlier. When I was standing, they proceeded to joke about my sudden incapacity in that age-old way men of all ages have, as if words might codify loss and change and time's betrayal. I joined in the joking. But what I really wanted was to go home and contemplate this latest fall, in the privacy of my apartment. The implications were clear: I would never again be an eater of salt; I would also never again get to my feet on my own. A part of my life had ended. But that didn't depress me. In fact, I felt almost as exhilarated as I had thirty-eight years earlier, when my body surrendered to the need to let go and I fell into life.

Almost four years have passed since I fell on the wet sidewalk of 14th Street. I suppose it wasn't a particularly memorable fall. It wasn't even particularly significant to anyone who had not once fallen into life. But it was inevitable, the first time I had let go into a time when it would no longer even be necessary to let go.

It was a fall that left me with the knowledge that I could no longer pick myself up. That meant I now needed the help of others as I had not needed their help before. It was a fall that left me burning with this strange passion for symmetry, this desire to balance my existence out. When the day comes, I want to be able to fall into my death as nakedly as I once had to fall into my life.

Do not misunderstand me. I am not seeking a way out of mortality, for I believe in nothing more strongly than I believe in the permanency of endings. I am not looking for a way out of this life, a life I continue to find immensely enjoyable—even if I can no longer pull myself to my own two feet. Of course, a good deal in my life has changed. For one thing, I am increasingly impatient with those who claim to have no use for endings of any sort. I am also increasingly embarrassed by the thought of the harshly critical adolescent I was, self-righteously convinced that the only way for a man to go to his end was kicking and screaming.

But these are, I suppose, the kinds of changes any man or woman of forty or fifty would feel. Middle-aged skepticism is as natural as adolescent acne. In my clearer, less passionate moments I can even laugh at my need for symmetry in beginnings and endings as well as my desire to see my own eventual death as a line running parallel to my life. Even in mathematics, let alone life, symmetry is sometimes too neat, too closed off from the way things actually work. After all, it took me a full month before I could bring myself to let go and fall into life.

I no longer talk about how to seize a doctrine of compensation from disease. I don't talk about it, but it still haunts me. In my heart, I believe it offers the only philosophy by which anyone can actually live. It is the only philosophy that strips away both spiritual mumbo jumbo and the procrustean weight of existential anxiety. In the final analysis, a man really is what he does.

Believing as I do, I wonder why I so often find myself trying to frame a perspective that will prove adequate to a proper sense of ending. Perhaps that is why I find myself sitting in a bar with a friend, trying to explain to him all I have learned from falling. "There must be a time," I hear myself tell him, "when a man has the right to stop thinking about falling."

"Sure," my friend laughs. "Four seconds before he dies."

In search of Jackson's Island

As a writer, I am a creation of disease. Most of my life before my confrontation with polio at the age of eleven seems distant and faded, like the pictures on our living room wall of my *shtetl* grandfather. There was a life before the polio. And there is no doubt that it was mine. But its significance has been diminished by what the polio wrought, as if, like the fading photograph of my grandfather, whose eyes stared out at me from his bearded skullcap-stroked *rebbe*'s face, its evocation of what is now "foreign" and "strange" is all that makes it interesting. Its distance from me is its greatest significance. The man I am today can find little meaningful relationship to that pre-polio past.

Yet that life, too, contains glimpses of the world to come. It offers points of departure in which I catch myself entering the world, such as that time when I was ten years old and ran away from home to place myself securely within Western myth and culture. I didn't know it at the time, but a flight from home that lasted no more than five or six hours made me spiritual brother to Moses and Oedipus and Don Quixote and Huck Finn and all those other heroes who haunt the imagination of Western man. They, too, ran away from home, and because they did they haunted my imagination, daring me to match their daring.

We find the figure everywhere—in the young man from the provinces fleeing his stodgy prospects for a world whose promise is that it will grow larger through his presence; in the bitter revolutionary seeking to destroy a society he cannot escape in a time he does not desire; in the sexual outlaw prepared to pay any price in order to fulfill passions he already knows are beyond true fulfillment.

For me and, I suspect, for many other boys, running away from home proved a curiously literary act. I would learn to read that time in my life as if it were a literary text, one foot in the fictions that helped create my aspirations, the other in the here and now of the world I lived in. At ten, the self and its hungers momentarily meshed, and I saw what writers had threatened I would see. It was, I now know, precisely the kind of time in which the extraordinary power of fiction touches a child.

My brief flight from home was no Joycean epiphany. It was simply a moment given me by an imagination nurtured on the clear envy that reading brings a child. The event itself took place late in October of 1943, a few weeks after I had taken to bed because of an ankle sprained while playing football. I had used my time out of school and in bed as I usually did, devouring book after book. And one of the books I read was *The Adventures of Tom Sawyer*.

Tom Sawyer remains the truest "boy's book" ever penned by an American author, perhaps the truest boy's book ever penned anywhere. It affected me more than anything else I had read. After my ankle healed and I returned to school, I felt haunted by Tom's schemes and boyishly American way of outwitting the adult world. I was particularly captivated by the scenes in which Tom and Huck and Joe Harper run away from St. Petersburg to savor the free-roaming, irresponsible life they discover on Jackson's Island.

My ankle healed. But even after I returned to my fifth-grade classroom in P.S. 80, I couldn't bring myself to go to the parks and ball fields after school. Whereas I once would literally have preferred a physical beating to missing a football game, I now wandered listlessly through the neighborhood, bobbing like a piece of cork through streets that had once spoken to my sense of adventure. Now they seemed shriveled and dry and emptied of purpose. I wanted a Jackson's Island of my own. I wanted to run away to a place where I, too, might stand free of the authority of adults.

I fancied myself the quintessential city boy. Provincial as only a child of New York can be, I possessed more than my share of that peculiarly urban ignorance of the world. I felt pity and scorn for anyone not fortunate enough to have been born and raised in this city. But to be a city boy inevitably meant seeing yourself as always on trial. The streets I loved so passionately provided the physical boundaries as well as the day-to-day challenges I had to get through. Reality in the city was overwhelmingly physical.

I loved Tom's St. Petersburg for the same reason I loved Hollywood westerns. Both embodied an America as different from my neighborhood as night was from day. Tom and his friends could run from an idyllic small town to the even more idyllic Jackson's Island. Their freedom, their ability to outmaneuver and outwit adult authority, filled me with envy. Dulled by my sense of opportunities lost, I wandered through streets grown mean and pedestrian. I lost my taste for sports. All I could think of was finding a Jackson's Island of my own.

Only I didn't have the broad sweep of the Mississippi to transport me beyond the power of adults interfering with my comings and goings. However attractive my dreams of drift and sun-drenched solitude, I was a cautious adventurer. Growing up in the city had made me instinctively distrustful of what my fifth-grade teacher, Miss Burge, called "your beautiful natural world."

Of course, I had studied geography. All children did back in 1943. I knew that "the lordly Hudson"—I first heard the phrase not from Paul Goodman, who used it as a title, but from the redoubtable Miss Burge—flowed a few miles west of my corner of the Bronx. It was there, but I couldn't remember having actually seen it. The only river I had seen was the insignificant flow of water that slipped, like a bashful suitor, through Bronx Park. Miss Burge insisted that that insignificant flow was the Bronx's own true river. Her word was good enough for me. But, river or stream, no highway to freedom was to be found on that trickle. No one had fled adult authority by floating down the Bronx River.

I couldn't head north either. Blocking the way to the rumored wealth of Westchester were the vast spaces of Woodlawn Cemetery. A decade later, when I was a junior in college, I would escort a woman I was trying to impress through that repository of nineteenth-century New York, searching for Melville's tomb. But at ten, cemeteries terrified me. On Saturday afternoon excursions to the movies, if a scene set in a cemetery flashed on screen I would bury my head, ostrichlike, against the back of the seat in front of me until I was assured the scene was over. Some seven or eight miles east was Orchard Beach, Robert Moses's contemptuous gift to our plebeian aspirations. From its sand-encrusted walks we gazed out over the cold gray waters of Pelham Bay and beyond to the Atlantic. But there was a war on. Beneath those waters, Nazi submarines hunted in wolf packs.

Tom Sawyer's river-split landscape was not mine. A city boy's Mississippi would have to be the IND subway line's D train. I would have to discover my Jackson's Island in those still mysterious regions people called "downtown" in 1943. Downtown was where I would search for freedom and indolence and danger. Downtown was where my dreams of independence would lead. Downtown would rid me of the heavy control of adults.

I slipped into the morning rush-hour throng lining the subway platform on 206th Street on a blustery late-October day. I was not running away with Moses or Don Quixote or Oedipus in mind. The models for my escape were Tom and Huck and Joe Harper. I knew I should have been standing in line with my friends in the schoolyard of P.S. 80. But, nervous and edgy as I was, Tom's example gave me heart. I was determined to maneuver my way past the power of adults as deftly as Tom and his friends had.

Inside the subway car, I sat down, convinced that every other passenger had guessed I was running away from home. I glanced from side to side, furtively, like a cornered animal certain that it is the focus of everybody's attention. That my fellow passengers sat or stood with their eyes closed or else tried to manipulate their newspapers so that they could follow a story was simply a ruse designed to catch me off guard. When the train pulled noisily into the 125th Street station, I jumped to my feet and, timing my dash to freedom to coincide with the hissing of the air brakes and the opening of the doors, split two rush-hour riders struggling for possession of the center pole. The train doors closed behind me, and I found myself on a station platform filled with a swarming mass of dark-skinned men and women. I took a deep breath, filled with relief. I was free.

For the next two hours, I forced myself to move through those streets against a brisk wind. I was seeking the butter softness of Tom Sawyer's Jackson's Island idyll in the streets of Harlem. Within the year, Harlem would witness a riot to be memorably recorded by yet another fictional runner, the unnamed narrator of Ralph Ellison's *Invisible Man*. But the Harlem through which I wandered on that windy October morning didn't strike me as dangerous. It wasn't particularly exotic, either. No, these streets were simply a part of New York where the careworn faces were black instead of white and where the gutters were a touch dirtier and the buildings a touch seedier than in the Bronx neighborhood from which I had journeyed. I passed old ladies walking their dogs. I made my way into Mount Morris Park. I climbed the iron steps of the fire watchtower so that I could gaze across all the mean streets of the city. The panorama seemed to peel the very life from these streets. But I could not find what I had come for. Jackson's Island was not to be discovered here.

Tired and bored, I made my way back to the subway station at 125th Street. I don't really know why I took the downtown local. Perhaps I was simply unwilling to admit defeat and make my sheepish return to Miss Burge and my classmates in the Bronx. I don't even know why I suddenly left the train when I spotted the sign announcing its arrival at the Museum of Natural History at 79th Street. I had been to the museum in April, on one of those wartime school excursions intended to enrich the lives of the children of New York's toiling masses. But in April I had been surrounded by thousands of other schoolchildren. Now I was alone. I had run away. Guilt touched me with its nervous electricity. I shivered. No matter what his intentions, I knew that a boy who had run away had set himself beyond the casual indiscretions of childhood.

Tom Sawyer's bucolic innocence is what I had expected to feel. I wanted to lie against a hogshead of tobacco with Huck Finn and smoke a corncob pipe. Instead, I felt guilty and lonely as I warily eyed the other visitors to the museum. Almost all of them were old, shopworn, oblivious to the adventure I sought and the growing sense of danger I felt. Mixed in with the old denizens of the museum were infant-laden carriages and strollers pushed by bored middle-aged women.

I drifted from exhibit to exhibit, searching the dioramas and the glass cases that housed stones and gems, to find some personal memento that might rekindle the courage and expectation with which I had started out that morning. I felt oppressed by age. Once the earth itself had been young. Now I walked through the museum with these tired remnants of New York, examining the skeletal remains of giant dinosaurs that had feasted on the green heaviness of this earth. I grew queasy, frightened. There was little of the bucolic to be found in these halls. Miss Burge's "beautiful natural world" was hostile and dangerous.

With each passing minute my trepidation grew. I felt lightheaded, the way I used to feel when I rummaged in my grandmother's heavily scented closets, seeking the secrets of that dark and death-ridden Europe my family had fled. Outside, the wind slapped against the museum's big windows. Imprisoned behind glass, nature was more threatening than soothing. The world seemed a giant cage, and from behind its prison bars it sent forth a rush of terror, like the whisper of imminent death. A shiver went through me. Quite suddenly, I felt overwhelmed, not with a sense of adventure but with responsibility for myself.

As I write this now, I tell myself I need a rhetoric of deflation, some comic recognition of childhood memories readers and writers share, some verbal gesture to present the moment as proper comedy. But that wasn't what I felt. I felt as if I had lost some vital part of myself. Sweating as if a fever were breaking, I sensed that Jackson's Island and all it represented had slipped permanently from my grasp. Nor was I surprised to hear my gasp of terror as I turned into the hall that held the giant war canoe. On the solidity of space that seemed frozen, the canoe plunged toward me, the eyes of its savage carved inhabitants staring into my terror. How vividly I remember those eyes. They threatened to follow me to the ends of the earth. From the thick elongated shadows I heard imaginary voices cry out, "Run! Run! Run!"

I wanted to run. To run forever. So intense was the threat of those carved warriors that I would have done anything to get away. Hunched down, as if prepared to charge the canoe and battle them hand-to-hand, I felt the panic within me explode. Defeat flooded my body with relief. I jumped to my feet, turned, and ran past the aged denizens of the museum, oblivious to the amazement on their withered faces as I fled back to the subway that would take me home.

I was the child of an America that has long since passed us by. This was the realization that would ultimately allow me, long after I had fled the museum, to explicate that moment in my life as studying the New Critics would teach me to explicate a text. The image remains fixed: a terrified boy, his dreams turned to nightmare, bursts wildly through the halls of the museum, discarding the husbanded mementos of nature's past for the cowardly relief of a subway ride back to the same Bronx neighborhood he had run from that morning. I still see myself, running toward even as I ran away. What I ran toward was the simple necessity of accepting responsibility for my life. Obviously, I didn't think of my panic-drenched flight from the museum in such grandiose terms when I was ten. I was much too busy running. But, like books, lives are read after their creation. Even at the risk of being charged with a certain psychological pomposity, I remain convinced that it is precisely such moments in our personal histories that reflect the lives we ultimately attempt to lead.

The only discovery I made on that windy late-October day was that I would find no Jackson's Island—not in the streets of Harlem, not in the inadequately lit Museum of Natural History, not even in the parks and playgrounds of my own Bronx neighborhood. For in the carved eyes of those wooden warriors I had somehow fixed on the dilemma that would plague me, just as it would plague every boy born into an America that sent us reeling in two contradictory directions. Each of us felt the need to run away and to seek his selfhood in the idyllic landscape of Jackson's Island at the same time that each of us struggled to stand his ground and to define a self that could exist beyond the confines of place. Now, as I look back at my brief and comic flight from home, it seems to me that those warriors splitting the heated museum air with their threat to engulf me were forcing me to break with the childish romance of freedom without consequence. They were telling me to run back home so that I could avoid the consequences of striking out too early on my own.

Even as a boy of ten I recognized my failure. Only I couldn't understand why I had failed. Not then. Eventually I would come to understand that my mistake was setting out to meet my fate at too early an age, before I allowed myself that gradual testing of experience which a child needs to become a legitimate adult. My instincts were certainly accurate. I needed time to claim what Whitman had claimed, time to loaf and invite my soul. Curiously enough, it was disease that would give me that time—two years in an upstate hospital which were brutally painful and yet functionally idyllic. When I was ten and ran away from home, I needed laziness. But the models I chose were inadequate. Tom and his friends lacked the balance that would have allowed me to understand that running away did not lead to discovering the authentic self in its day-to-day world. Illness would teach me that I also needed to stand my ground.

To stand my ground was the kind of lesson experience alone could teach me. The fact is that every boy I knew shared the fantasy of finding a Jackson's Island of his own. It was the dream that sent us every Saturday afternoon, hands clutching the thin dime that offered us admission to the inner sanctum of fantasy, to the Mosholu Theater, where we could sit through six hours of cartoons and double or triple features and serialized weekly adventures, only to stagger out like drunken bums, still not in possession of Jackson's Island.

In 1943, running away was a metaphor for the process by which a boy came of age. The newspapers and radio were filled with stories of thirteen- or fourteen-year-old boys who had run away from home, lied about their age, and enlisted in the army, navy, or marines. While few boys I knew actually ran away, most considered it, pondering the immensity of the vast spaces we were told were ours by right of being American-born. But if thinking about running away was acceptable, doing it was certain to bring the stigma of cowardice. For chief among the lessons America was busily impressing on us that wartime year was that anyone who rejected the need to stand his ground might also endanger the process by which a boy was transformed into a man.

And if reading *Tom Sawyer* had pulled me into the boy's fantasy of ridding myself of the authority and demands of the adult world, I also read other things. The daily headlines in the *News* and the *Mirror* forced me to confront what was actually happening in the world. Those headlines shouted at me, told me how brutally demanding reality could be. You didn't run away from reality. Its demands were too inexorable, its reach overwhelming.

Much has been written about the Second World War, but very little of that writing focuses on what it was like to be a young boy during those years. This is understandable enough. Boys were spectators, peripheral to the action until they grew into men. If they counted at all, they counted as cheerleaders for what the newspapers and radio termed "the national effort." And yet, whether in my Bronx or in Detroit or Des Moines or some sleepy town on the banks of the Mississippi that looked like the clone of Tom's St. Petersburg a hundred years earlier, boys thought about the war in 1943 as they thought about nothing else.

For we were the children of the war's contradictions. We

prayed for the war to end, for our brothers and uncles and cousins to return safe and victorious. And in the next breath, filled with the silent fervor of our own burgeoning manhood, we prayed for the war to last long enough that we, too, might test ourselves in it. We were, I suspect, the most war-obsessed generation of boys ever to live in these United States. In the headlines, on the radio, in the newsreels before which we surfaced from our fantasies at the movies for a few minutes every Saturday afternoon, we traced our fate in the world's fate. For it was our own fate we hungered after. Those headlines graphed our emotional state. We longed for the ending that was no ending. We sat transfixed by the heroism we were told was ours to emulate. We absorbed the rage and determination that screamed from the well-preserved, stubble-ridden face of Robert Taylor as he prepared to meet his death, machine gun still blazing away at the swarming Japanese, in the movie *Bataan*.

We didn't know it at the time, but we were being pulled into the heart of the myths of Western man. Incipient warriors all (were ten-year-old German boys our clones, enthralled by the same visions in different uniforms?), we did not need Homer to sing of the heroic exploits before the gates of Troy or the prophet Samuel to describe the battles of Saul and David. We kept scrapbooks filled with maps and dispatches cut from the papers. For our sake alone, enormous battles were encapsulated into brief paragraphs. We pored over jagged, curlicued lines like waxen-faced Talmudists, knowing that arrows facing one way meant *we* had won and arrows facing another meant *we* were running away in ignominious retreat.

What obsessed us was the performance of *our* American "boys." We were the emotional proprietors of the struggles of soldiers who stood where we ourselves wanted someday to stand. And our focus on the American soldier's performance grew even more concentrated after news of a defeat. That was when our sense of realism about the war clashed with the heroic image of the grimly handsome Robert Taylor going to his noble, machine gun–blazing death. We lived within the fires of our own hopes and fears. Myth and reality alike catechized us in the expectations of the nation. We *knew* American men didn't run away. And even when the arrows testified to a different story, we had no choice but to remain believers. We weren't experienced enough to understand the vast and unending public relations campaign in which belief and reality meshed.

We measured success and failure according to the standards taught us by an America we simply never questioned. If our myths insisted American men had no right to run away, well, then, they had no right. What else was it that sent me bolting in terror from the museum? Why else would I accuse myself over and over of "bolting like a jackrabbit" when I had never seen a jackrabbit in the streets and parks of the Bronx? (In accepting the myths of our America, we embraced the language and landscape of those myths.) If, like every other boy I knew, I wanted to find my own dreamed-of Jackson's Island, I wanted even more to be tough enough to stand my ground. We early on learned to thrust the world into which we had been born against those fantasies designed to teach us how to avoid its consequences. In the final analysis, that was why I had run away. It was also why I had run away from running away.

Even the games we played in 1943 took their structures from the imminence of manhood. How singular were the lessons we were expected to absorb. We were being groomed for our fate, learning how a man behaved and what he had to do to earn the approbation of his peers. On furiously hot summer afternoons, when the air was so thick and heavy that none of us could stand even the prospect of playing ball on Mosholu Parkway or on one of the rock-strewn lots that could still be found in the north Bronx in 1943, we would gather beneath a tree in the angular yard behind the apartment building in which we lived to corner our fantasies with card games.

Tom Sawyer would have understood the motives, if not the specific games. We played a game called Go Fish and we played boyish variations of poker, betting pebbles or sticks or even pennies we had "fished," with bamboo poles and chewing gum, from beneath the subway gratings. But the game we played with the passionate dedication of young religious novitiates being inducted into the intricate mysteries of faith was the game we called Knucks.

At this point in time I can remember absolutely nothing about what the rules of the game were or exactly how one went about winning or losing. What I can remember is that whenever we played Knucks, I would envision myself as a POW in some Nazi detention camp. And I also remember that the friends I played with confessed to similar fantasies. But my strongest memory is of what happened after the game ended. One won or lost by points, and losers were expected to hold out their hands, fists clenched, so that the winners could scrape their knuckles with the closed deck of cards. (The number of scrapings had to do with the number of points by which one lost.)

It was a sadistic game, and we often emerged from a morning spent playing Knucks with knuckles scraped raw or bleeding. But it was also a game into which my pre-polio self poured its expectations of what would be expected of me. To demonstrate endurance was important. It is not, apparently, a game boys in New York play today. One can understand that in a city in which nine-year-olds have access to real guns and knives, knuckle-scraping is as much of an anachronism as box ball or King or a game we played with a penknife called Land.

I can only assume that Knucks flourished during the war because it provided boys with a way of testing their ability to stand their ground, to see whether they were "men enough" to endure pain. A boy who held out his clenched fist knew that he could wince or cry out or weep or even scream in pain as his knuckles were scraped. The only thing he couldn't do was run away and not face his punishment "like a man."

However sadistic it was, Knucks provided a ritual against which we could test ourselves. It allowed us to link our fate to the fate of "our boys" overseas. We saw ourselves as being tested, in much the same way as the men fighting in Sicily and the South Pacific were being tested. The demands of the war would prove to be more persuasive than the fantasy of finding our own Jackson's Island. Standing your ground was more imperative than liberating yourself from adult power. However striking such a dichotomy may seem today, it was as natural as the air we breathed in 1943.

After the war, the dichotomy grew ever more pronounced, until the knot binding running away to standing one's ground unraveled. It unraveled first in our own lives. We simply ceased being boys. Then it unraveled throughout the nation. Postwar America was a profoundly different nation from the country that had fought and won the Second World War. It was not merely that for the twenty years following the war's end the United States would possess more power than any other nation in history. It was something more profound, something that had to do with the cohesiveness we had possessed as a people being lost in the acquisition of power.

The Second World War imposed on this nation a sense of unity that was both political and cultural. The nation's young were what the nation's myths told them to be. But for all the much-heralded conformity of the 1950s, it was during those years that the national myths proved increasingly incapable of holding the allegiance of the young. The national ethos, which had seemed so natural to my generation, grew increasingly remote from the students I taught in the 1960s and 1970s—as remote, I now believe, as the world that bound the feet of the infant Oedipus or cast the infant Moses into the waters of the Nile was to me. It would ultimately be easier for the students I taught during the sixties and seventies to understand the Wars of the Roses than to understand the country that had fought and won the Second World War.

It is not a proposition I can prove. On the surface, at least, my students resembled me closely. They had been born and raised in New York—usually, like me, in one of the outer boroughs. They were not prepared to see themselves as standing at the center of the world. Their skepticism was as pronounced as my own, they moved warily through what had not yet tested them, and they assumed the validity of their own experience, if for no other reason than that they had nothing else to depend on.

Given those similarities, I would have expected them to avoid the dangers of dogmatic thinking. Even more, I would have expected them not to inflate the self at the expense of reality, to keep their distance both from what endorsed their passions and from what denied them. They should have been less angry than my own generation, for they had begun their march toward adulthood, not during the Second World War, but in an America presided over by the fatherly Dwight David Eisenhower as if it were a family business waiting to be passed on to its preselected heirs.

I do not want to add to the chorus of indictments of the 1950s as a boring, quiescent decade, since it seems to me to have been neither quiescent nor boring. But it was certainly a decade during which America changed—a change discernible in the differences between the myths that shaped my aspirations and those that shaped the aspirations of my students. In the sixties my students would take to the streets to protest a war in which we Americans had assumed the role of invaders. And my students had never felt the accusation in the eyes of carved warriors in the Museum of Natural History. They did not dream of Jackson's Island. Even the communes in northern Oregon and Vermont to which a few of them would ultimately flee had as their purpose, not the liberation of the self from the pressures society deemed important, but the leveling of the world. They hungered for a democratization of the spirit in which spirit itself would be vanquished. When they ran away, their purpose was social and political. They ran to Canada, they ran to Sweden; they ran from the draft and from an unjust war.

The violence of their encounters was certainly more formidable than that of ten-year-old boys testing their endurance by scraping their knuckles. Of course, all myths of flight are saturated with violence. The Oedipus who runs away from Corinth carries within himself the desire to stand alone against a hostile world. His lonely sense of righteousness—the pain of what he has given up—is what leads to his slaying of his biological father, Laius. The Moses who seeks holiness before the burning bush on Mount Horeb stands on the edge of nightmare: He is about to run toward the Egypt he once ran from.

When my students echoed black militants, insisting that violence was as American as cherry pie, they spoke from inside a culture in which the threat of violence had been absorbed into the coming-of-age process even more thoroughly than it had been in the America of the Second World War. Violence had probably always been fascinating to American adolescents. Tom and Huck and Joe Harper, whose appeal was so closely linked to their physical innocence, would ultimately evolve into an adulthood formed by the ever-present American potential for physical violence. I have always felt that *Huckleberry Finn*, a book in which the childish violence of *Tom Sawyer* threatens to spin out of control, is Twain's acknowledgment that he overemphasized the innocence of his boys.

The end of the Second World War brought an end to the possibility of such innocence. It made running away to a Jackson's Island even more idyllic than Twain intended, turning it into a moronic television sitcom such as *Gilligan's Island*. It is not by accident that contemporary writers feel the necessity to rewrite *Huck Finn*, to make the novel's violence more consequential. For when the Second World War ended and America emerged as the most powerful nation on this devastated planet, Tom and his friends had to be replaced. Their boyish faces, reflections of an optimism and goodwill that would disappear from the nation's life, would give way to the sullen indifference that stamps the face of Marlon Brando as he leads a motorcycle gang through small-town America in the film *The Wild Ones*. Brando leads his gang from nowhere to nowhere. His fellow motorcyclists are neither adults nor children. They possess adult faces, but they are adults caught in a time warp. Their faces reflect the imprimatur of what separates the America of my students from my own America. Action and age have been divorced. Mounted on their machines, Brando and his cohorts roar through the American landscape. But this is a land so impersonal that it shrinks from the freedom it should offer. Like the grown-up children of Kerouac's *On the Road*, they travel not through geographic space but through their own needs. For all their whooping and boisterous celebration of the open spaces, they remind one of infants mewling for their teething rings.

In the 1950s, the landscape filled up and the empty places disappeared into the bocks and doctoral dissertations that told us how American culture had been formed out of the nation's sense of a limitless geography. Even as we told ourselves that the empty landscape could still be found everywhere, the young were insisting that all roads led back into the questing self. Like American lives, American myths had become mechanized. Raft and river had been replaced by car and motorcycle and interstate highway. Running away was just another media event, as receptive to the embrace of cameras and crews and directors as the Miss America Beauty Pageant.

For the power of myth had shriveled, as had the power of those fictions toward which boys like me once aspired. Jackson's Island was a refuge from adulthood, more idea than reality. I never found a Jackson's Island of my own. But for years it remained at the center of my imagination, a promise of authenticity. What did one's private refuge matter in a nation given over to fantasies that were wholesaled? Soap operas, game shows, fundamentalist religions with televised preachers, sports that were packaged and repackaged and then videotaped so that they seemed as spontaneous as death, political gurus who cornered fashionability, camps for "adults" in which for a few thousand dollars every man could spend a week pretending he was Joe DiMaggio and every woman could play at being Marilyn Monroe—these were the addictions of a culture which no longer discriminated about age. Once the fantasies had belonged to children. After the war, they were given over to the needs of adults. Who among us can deprive ourselves of any dream?

The individual who runs away has become the bearer not of a quest for autonomy but of the pervasive boredom of hanging around. Not that the young no longer run away. On evening television, they dutifully smile into the cameras waiting to greet them at the Port Authority Bus Terminal in New York or at the Los Angeles International Airport. To dream of Jackson's Island today is simply to reflect the neon tinsel of the Minnesota Strip.

For in this America no one, apparently, worries about standing his ground. But in 1943, America still possessed scale and proportion. Ambition was simpler, a way of defining oneself as an American. I feel distant from the boy I was then, as I feel distant from the grandfather staring down at me from his place on the wall. Like my *shtetl* grandfather, I would never be modern enough for this world.

But the world had a way of catching up with our ambitions and of leading us beyond our failures. In 1943, a ten-year-old boy could still run toward even as he ran away. For that was when the dream of Jackson's Island still burned with the promise of autonomy, a promise an American boy might discover anywhere.

Homage to Barney Ross

Ten years ago, convinced I had used up whatever literary capital remained in my life, I set out to change direction as a writer. Determined to become more inventive and less autobiographical, I would force myself to shake loose from the obligations of memory. Other than a short book about Edmund Wilson, all of the five books I had written up to that point in my career were conditioned by my need to sort out the events of my own life and give them meaning.

All autobiographical writers face a time when those events threaten to overwhelm the language the writer uses to shape them and give his life definition. The life set down in words threatens to become more real than the life that exists in memory alone.

I felt that my own life had become too retrospective, too literary, when I finished an autobiographical meditation on the situation facing American men after a decade and a half of a resurgent feminism. Armed with my determination to take my literary leave of the autobiographical self, I wrote a novel about the rise and fall of a labor leader. I was in the middle of another novel when, early in 1985, I wrote an essay for the "About Men" column of the *New York Times Magazine*, an essay I intended as a brief coda to my book on manhood.

The subject of the essay was the price I had paid for the attack of polio that left me crippled in body and enraged in spirit at the age of eleven. Seemingly against my conscious will, I found myself once again drawn into my encounter with disease. Memory smashed against my determination not to write about myself, thrust me yet once more against the central event in my life, an event I wrote about because I still could not wholly accept it as mine.

That I had written about my polio before—my first book, *The Long Walk Home*, was intended to put the effects of polio behind me—simply made me angrier at the prospect of writing about it again. But no matter how angry I might be, no matter how much I harangued myself about my inability to let go of what could not be changed and to write about something other than the life I called my own, it was as if only by again writing about my lifetime war with a polio virus could I regain control of that life, as if my past were a series of sketches that could be erased and redrawn at will.

The virus had claimed more than my legs with which to feed its hunger. I was a writer whose imagination was literally "disease-ridden." Disease gave even as it took, a gift the imagination offered itself. Even as it created the bleak prospects of a difficult future, it fed the imagination fantasies designed to keep those prospects at arm's length. And even as I lay in a country hospital and the virus continued its march from my toes to my stomach, I learned that I could let my mind drift off into fantasized triumphs. The ability to imagine myself whole in body and triumphant in spirit was born during the early days and nights of my disease. As life itself hung in the balance and the doctors dealing with my case debated whether or not to place me in an oxygen tent, I discovered that an imaginary life could take the place of a real life stalled dead in its tracks.

While the consequences of polio were primarily physical—I would never again be able to walk without braces running the full length of my legs, and crutches in my hands—my disease had profound nonphysical ramifications from the beginning. Even as it insisted that I learn to "face reality," disease fed me fantasies. Reality was "tough," offering the satisfaction of knowing that one had to earn survival in what I soon learned to call "the real world." Fantasy, on the other hand, allowed me to reshape my life to images of my own choosing. Until I was sixteen, reality had the smell of death and decay, while fantasy carried me through long, tedious afternoons and empty nights. "Our only health is the disease," wrote T. S. Eliot. He might have been speaking about mortality, but when I read that line I could not help thinking he was talking about fantasy.

Until I met up with my virus, I was a monotonously average eleven-year-old boy. And I suppose it was only natural that the fantasies to which my disease gave birth were conventional. No dreams of erotic women or exotic lands for me. I was a city boy, and my imaginative fantasies were as constricted as my ambitions were decisive. Lying in bed or staring out from my bedroom window at the street below, I would wrap myself in dreams generated by my past life. I would recreate my shattered body into the body of a fighter or a ball player.

"Normal" boys are forced to surrender such childish ambitions by the time they are fifteen. A moment would have come for me, as it came for the friends I grew up with, when I simply realized my hands weren't quick enough or my feet shifty enough or my eyes keen enough to be a professional athlete. But I was no longer "normal." Monotonously average, yes—but a monotonously average cripple who needed fantasy to overcome the straitjacketing boredom of disease. I was no Stephen Hawking dancing to the rhythms of the universe in his mind. The pictures in my mind were still of the undevastated body.

As I daydreamed during the hours my friends were in school or at play in the fields of the Bronx, I felt myself buffeted between the reality of useless legs and the dream of physical grace all adolescents cherish. It was as if I had been caught, exposed on an open plain, by a violent eruption of wind and rain slashing against my dream of independent selfhood. Fantasy was the only shelter I could see against the disintegration threatened by that storm.

An alternative life is no less vivid for being imaginary. Fantasies anchored to imaginary bodies helped stave off my inevitable confrontation with the future until I was strong enough to face that future with hope. Fantasy allowed me to try on roles as I had once tried on clothing in summer shopping expeditions with my mother to the Lower East Side wilds of Orchard Street. By the time I returned from the upstate hospital, at the age of thirteen, the nerves in my legs were dead and the muscles withered and atrophied into sticks of flesh and bone. But my skill as an athlete exploded in images so strong they could leave me gasping with pleasure. I could grab at triumph with a quick and certain imaginative touch. As my once-lean frame spread into bedridden fat, my imagination created a body for me that could have been no more muscularly symmetrical had it been sculpted by Praxiteles.

As "the real world" grew more difficult and less appealing, I bombarded myself with images of muscular prowess. Conversely, the triumphs I imagined made my actual life as a cripple more real as well as more acceptable. I sensed that my escape from the future was only temporary, a marking-time which would someday end. And I never lost the ability to distinguish real from unreal, not even when I was caught up in the most delicious fantasies.

For the ability to escape *into* did not mean the ability to escape *from*. Fantasy had consequences that paralleled the consequences of disease itself. I had to learn to take the weight of my own imagination. And not even an active imagination could free itself from the demands of the specific. I might learn to deal with the way things were by calling up visions of the way they should have been. The ache of talents lost and ambition mocked sealed me within the bitter recognition that disease takes more than the parts of one's body.

Before I took sick, I had done my share of fighting in street and schoolyard. Such fighting was a condition of existence, like attending school or playing curb ball. Not that I boxed. No one I knew boxed. Boxing was a demonstration of finesse and skill; fighting was a dream of simple demolition. Its essence was hitting and getting hit.

I fantasized about fighting because I worshiped power. And I worshiped it most when it was absent from my own life. Adults might be hypocritical enough to pretend that power was subservient to style or grace or courage. But everything I witnessed in the city told me that power had nothing at all to do with style or grace or courage. It had to do with hitting harder and enduring more. And it meant that you were "better" than your opponent.

At nine and ten, I spent endless summer hours discussing different fighting styles, matching this one's straight-up come-at-you approach to another's bob-and-weave. Furiously shadowboxing in the overbearing sun, we would show off to each other. I loved those childhood demonstrations of footwork and agility. I would work my way through what we called "the moves" as if I were an unmarked Errol Flynn strutting his flashy, ironic way through the film *Gentleman Jim*. But such showmanship had nothing to do with fighting. To be a fighter, you had to hit and be willing to get hit in return.

Philosophers of physical nuance, we city boys followed the lead of strength and power as trustingly as a lion cub follows its mother. We insisted on knowing what we would receive for what we would be called upon to give. Imposing your will on an opponent was as important in a street fight as it was in the broadcast Friday night main events at Madison Square Garden. And we needed no interpreter to tell us what the announcer at the Garden meant when he urged each fighter to do his best until one of them "emerges triumphant."

To emerge triumphant was the goal in fighting, as it was in life. Long before he reputedly said it, my friends and I understood Vince Lombardi's famous dictum, "Winning isn't everything. It's the only thing." Lombardi was saying that rules and strategies and techniques mattered only when you won. The object of a fight was to make your opponent admit he had had enough. No amount of rhetoric about sportsmanship or fair play (in which we all claimed to believe) could change the way we looked at the world: In a world divided between winners and losers, it was better to be a winner.

Skill as a fighter was, then, distinct from style or grace or courage. It was also, like long division, measurable and teachable. Given average physical coordination, any boy could learn to handle himself. Who among us does not remember those movies in which the father or uncle or older brother takes the bookish young boy, who has just undergone a beating at the hands of the local bully, into the yard or behind some junk-strewn lot to teach him "the manly art of self-defense"?

Perhaps because anyone could learn to fight, no one I knew worshiped fighters as we worshiped other athletes. At eight, I knew what Joe DiMaggio or Pete Reiser was hitting on any given day. I knew Whitlow Wyatt's earned run average as well as I knew my address. I learned how to do percentages by dividing the number of passes Sid Luckman or Sammy Baugh attempted by the number completed. Such statistics fueled the order of my world. But a fighter's statistics were meaningless. His weight, height, arm reach, the number of his knockouts, the size of his biceps, all lacked the true distinctions of measurement. His skill might be definable, his endurance visible. But statistics measured nothing. Fighters were neither complex nor mythic. The integrity of fighting lay in its availability to all.

It was probably inevitable that I anchored fantasies of bodily resurrection to fighting, for the weak dream of being strong and the powerless dream of gaining power. Even as I lay stiff in bed after the initial onslaught of my virus, the strength draining from my body, I was learning to stave off the reality of what was happening to me. My fantasies needed no strategies for survival. The only questions concerned capacity. In fantasy, as in life, who did what to whom meant something. I was not a professional fighter. I would not have to approach life through the ethos of the fighter. I simply had to turn fantasy loose, to allow it to reconcile irreconcilable opposites. If, in real life, fighters could be crude and punchy and even cowardly, that could easily be folded into the larger need. What, after all, did real life have to do with the dream of power generated by dead legs?

My fantasies about fighting were always predicated on regaining the power of my legs. They did not soothe and they were not really dramatic. No other performance can match the spectacle of two men of roughly the same size, each of them naked to the waist with hands balled into gloved fists, trying to destroy each other in a roped-off square known as a ring. And yet I never thought of fighting as dramatic. Only ritual sacrifice possesses the shocking imaginative appeal boxing can claim. I know that now. But I didn't know it then. I created myself in my dreamer's eye as a fighter because I wanted to seize the power of my weakness from the death of my legs.

What I sought from dreams of fighting was not what I sought from my other fantasies of athletic prowess: It wasn't the resurrection of movement I craved, nor was it the almost unbearably sweet memory of the tingling sensation in my wrists as bat connected with ball. I depended upon my fantasies about fighting for something deeper, a sense of myself as still possessing the very power whose absence threatened to destroy me even as I dreamed, spurred on by my weakness. Pretending I was a fighter promised to freeze the drift into helplessness, to give me back a voice in my fate. What other fantasy could allow me to see myself once again imposing my presence on my world?

But if I wanted power because of the death of my legs, I still maintained, even in fantasy, a young boy's respect for form and propriety. There was an order to fighting, just as there was a certain propriety to dreaming about it. It wasn't supposed to be excessively dramatic or even one-sided. Even fantasized triumphs had to be earned.

And fighters were certainly not role models for me. They were reputed to be "dumb," products of the very streets on which we shadowboxed in emulation of their skills. Even before I took sick with polio, I wanted to escape those streets—not because they were mean or poor or dangerous, but precisely because they were none of these. They simply marked off the point at which I, and people like me, had come into the world. And where one feels at home is not usually where one wants to see oneself entering the future.

But my very familiarity with fighting made fighters themselves a more ordinary part of the landscape. I did not worship fighters when I was a boy growing up in the Bronx. I did not collect cards with pictures of boxers on them as I greedily hoarded cards with pictures of baseball players, holding on to my collection with all the greed and avarice of a Chicago commodities broker betting on the future of pork bellies. Baseball players were gods to my eleven-year-old eyes; fighters were skilled craftsmen.

The sole exception to this was the great Barney Ross. But even with Ross, my admiration was not linked to his accomplishments as a fighter—by the time I became conscious of fighting as a sport, Ross had long since retired—but to the fact that he had been held up to me as the very model of a *mensch*, a man who had performed well within the context of that powerful if self-referential sentimentality of Jewish American urban life.

In a peculiar way, Ross came to embody for me the virtue of resistance to fate, even when I sensed that the fate had been sealed, stamped, and certified as unalterable by a power beyond anything I could imagine or believe in. His story was not that unusual. Ross was one of those gifted Jewish lightweights and flyweights and welterweights who emerged from the ghettos of Philadelphia and New York and Chicago during the 1920s and 1930s. Like Benny Leonard and Abe Attel and Lew Tendler, his skills as a fighter had made urban Jews more willing to assume American ambitions.

I met Barney Ross about a month before I met my virus. And the two meetings, perhaps as a remnant of an overheated imagination, remain linked in my mind. When I met him, Ross was not only no longer a fighter, he was a war hero who had been wounded during the island fighting in the Pacific and whose picture kissing the American ground on his return from overseas had been plastered across every newspaper in America. And Ross was a friend of my Uncle Morris's.

My uncle came to this country in 1920 as a boy of thirteen. I used to love to listen to his stories of arriving on the Lower East Side and of becoming acquainted with how things were done in America. I suspect his Americanization was actually similar to the process endured by hundreds of thousands of immigrants, Jew and Gentile, from Eastern Europe. If anything set him apart from the vast majority of his fellows, it was his peculiar amalgam of a passion for gambling and unswerving devotion to trade unionism. And in nothing did my uncle show off the success of his Americanization more than in his ability to live openly with his contradictions. I can still remember him making his way to Belmont Racetrack on Saturday mornings, the Communist *Daily Worker* and the horseplayer's *Morning Telegraph* rolled together in his right hand, the one offering him a line on the world, the other a line on the horses. And to this day I relish the memory of the sight of my Uncle Morris carefully tying an expensive and overly loud silk tie into a neat knot so that he would look suitably distinguished walking the picket line in the fur district.

During the Depression, when there was neither work for a talented cutter of mink nor a picket line that needed his ministrations, my uncle would often walk from the fur market on Seventh Avenue in the Twenties to Stillman's Gym on Eighth Avenue between 57th and 58th Streets. My uncle already possessed something of a reputation as a skilled handicapper of horses and fighters. A devoted regular of the Friday night fights at the Garden, and a more than occasional spectator at the fights at St. Nicholas Arena and Sunnyside Gardens, my uncle believed in watching the fighters he was considering betting on. "You watch a real good fighter train," he was fond of telling me, "and you can pretty much figure if the man is up to your needs."

One morning in 1934, my uncle found himself in Stillman's. He had come there to watch Barney Ross train for his title defense against the famed Fargo Express, Billy Petrolle. Ross was working out on the body bag in the upstairs room at Stillman's. Except for Ross and my uncle, the room was empty. My uncle watched carefully as Ross pounded away at the bag, sweat pouring from his face. Resting a moment, Ross turned to my uncle and asked, "Can you clock for me? Three minutes and stop." My uncle nodded. Whatever politics he might claim, when it came to betting his money my uncle was a true high-risk capitalist. An intelligent man, he understood, took a good look at what he was putting his money on. The working-class millennium was for the future. For the present, there was the question of how much he could afford to bet on Ross. "I see him sweat easy. I see he's loose. I figure there's no way Petrolle is going to take Barney. Where the hell is Fargo anyway?"

Ross went on to beat Petrolle. But he couldn't beat the wounds he suffered in the Pacific fighting. Those wounds left him battered in body. More important, they left him more bruised in spirit than the terrible beating he took at the hands of the great black fighter Henry Armstrong, when he lost his welterweight title in May of 1938, where for fifteen rounds, outboxed and outpunched, Ross simply offered himself and his title up before the New York fight mob in the Madison Square Bowl on Long Island City.

I don't know how my uncle arranged it. But we were going to meet Ross in front of Yankee Stadium on a Sunday afternoon. At that time, the prospect of accompanying my uncle to the Stadium was an almost unimaginable pleasure. We took a taxi—in itself a treat for me—stopping first in front of a candy store on Tremont Avenue, where my uncle worked out an eight-team parlay with the resident bookie. I was handed over to the man working the counter, who fed me an endless stream of pennies so that I could play the baseball pinball machine while my uncle "does his business in back."

At the Stadium we lingered outside, part of the good-natured

Sunday afternoon family crowd. It was June, not yet halfway through the season. But it was wartime baseball we were scheduled to see. In 1944, the Yankees were going nowhere. In 1944, metaphors and old truths were as useless as all other appeals to the ordinary and tested. The war stood expectation on its head. It was a star-crossed time, a season in which the St. Louis Browns, led by a pitcher with a quintessentially American name, Nelson Potter, could lay claim to superiority over the Yankees and Tigers and Red Sox. In 1944, even an eleven-year-old boy understood he would have to take his pleasure where he could.

Among the pleasures I was determined to take was watching batting practice. No matter how inept such wartime players as Mike Milosevich and Ed Levy and Bud Metheny might be, I insisted on watching batting practice. At eleven, I was a far more serious student of hitting a baseball than of math or history. But despite my entreaties, my uncle insisted we would wait outside the Stadium. "Barney's a hero," he said. "He deserves we should wait."

Disgruntled, I stood next to my uncle until he suddenly pushed me forward. "There he is!" he said excitedly. "There's Barney!"

A medium-sized man, perhaps five foot seven, limped toward us, wearing dark glasses, carrying a white cane, and dressed in a marine uniform overflowing with ribbons. The four or five men surrounding him moved to his hesitant rhythm. He shuffled forward as if he were about to enter a bath and was testing the temperature of the water with his toe. At first I thought he was blind. But he wasn't blind, just cautious. And he was frightened. I could sense that. He was far more frightened than he had been that night in Long Island City when he withstood barrage after barrage from Armstrong. He had lost a title then. Now he looked like a man who was all punched out, a man who felt himself in danger of losing his soul. My uncle held me at arm's length in front of Barney

Ross. I searched his face. I wanted to see in it the face of a hero. But what I saw was a high-cheekboned Eastern European Jew, a face as familiar to me as the leaves on the trees of Mosholu Parkway. I wanted to see in that face some secret experience that had transformed an ordinary man into a *mensch*. I saw only a tired man, stripped of defiance, stripped even of the determination and endurance and courage my uncle had seen that night Ross lost his title to Armstrong. "He was all punched out, Barney was," my uncle told me. "I see it from the third round on. Only he takes it. A terrible beating. And he keeps on coming, the way you got to do."

"Nice seeing you, Moe," Ross said, shaking hands with my uncle.

"This here's my nephew, Barney." My uncle pushed me even closer to Ross.

"How are you, kid?" The hand was out again, awaiting my acceptance. It felt soft and tender, not like what I had imagined the hand of a fighter would be. Suddenly Barney Ross smiled—a remarkably open smile in which he shed terror and fear and pain because, for this single moment, they meant nothing. He winked. He and I were conspirators together. "Ask your uncle to tell you how I handled Petrolle. Just keep on coming. Ain't that the way?"

That was forty-five years ago. I met Barney Ross and my virus within a month of each other. And I still find myself pleased at the parallels such chance encounters make available in an individual's life. Just keep on coming. Not a Socratic aphorism. But not bad advice, either, for someone suddenly finding himself crippled. Even if my way would be, at first, to keep on coming in my dreams and fantasies. Easy advice to follow. Anyway, fighters are not supposed to be philosophers. They are not paid to give memorable advice. It is enough when they give us memorable images.

Still, *just keep on coming* offers a simple justice. Even in memory. And a quiet rhetoric. After all, Barney Ross had been a champion. Better still, in my uncle's eyes and in mine, he had been a *mensch*, a word which still suggests to me a man made human when his power and skill are stripped away and he is left with nothing more than his sense of obligation and his endurance. And the challenge of whatever dreams remain.

I could tell real from false even at the age of eleven. And I knew that the tears in my eyes as we left Barney Ross and my uncle led me into the Stadium were not for the former champion and not for the war hero with the ribbons on his chest and not even for the consummate *mensch* of my uncle's insistence. This latest beating, I sensed, was far worse than anything Barney Ross had endured in the ring or in the streets of Chicago. My tears were for a man whose time was over. Barney Ross had lost.

I didn't know it then, but I would lose, too. Only fantasy would help carry me through, would help me stave off payment for that loss until I could patch myself up—the doctors and nurses and physical therapists would teach me, among other things, to call it rehabilitation—and face the consequences. In "the real world." And "realistically."

But I would lose. And in losing I would discover that a life, any life, is not merely the sum total of the conditions creating it. Losing one's legs to a virus was arbitrary. Being shot up in the Pacific was arbitrary. Time and circumstance had doomed me to the anguish of unfulfilled aspirations. No matter how trivial it seemed, no matter how adolescent it sounded, I would forever find my imagination ambushed by the "What if?" of my life. Time and circumstance had doomed Barney Ross, too.

The man I met on that warm June Sunday afternoon remains for me as bruised and battered in his soul as he was in his body. The war had taken his reality, had forced him to acknowledge that it was no longer enough to have been a champion, to be known as a *mensch*. I wonder now what fantasies kept him going during those years of pain and anguish that were to follow. Did he dream of old triumphs in the streets of Chicago? Did he hammer away at memories of a past no longer his in order to keep the unasked-for future at a distance?

Of course, I had no idea that Barney Ross was already a morphine addict when I met him, that pain racked his body and soul, that he would soon voluntarily commit himself to the government drug hospital in Lexington, Kentucky. But if I had known he was an addict it would have meant little to me. I hurt not for the man but for the defeat he had suffered. Vulnerability was not a word anyone used in 1944, but there was enough of it around. It was part of being human, of acknowledging what the world could do to you.

I would never get over my hunger to set right what I cannot fully accept even today. And that, I suspect, is not only why I am a writer but why I am condemned to shape and reshape that past, as if I can snatch an eleven-year-old boy's legs from my imagination. But I can't. I will never walk again. I will never run again. I will never hit a baseball again. I will never fight again.

And if, as I write once again about my encounter with the virus, I no longer need to fantasize my way out of what I want to avoid, I have at least learned to chart my debts and to acknowledge my hungers. However adolescent, they remain mine. Fantasy proved a gift both of and for the disease-ridden imagination. I owe my virus that much. For it was the disease-ridden imagination that recognized that before the day came that I could claim myself, I would have to claim all my imaginary selves. And I like to hope, too, that Barney Ross, *mensch* that he was, allowed himself to slip off into unknown futures built on the glory of the past, that he somehow managed to protect the breathtaking power of becoming what he needed to become.

Taking it

After I took sick with polio in the summer of 1944, even geography changed. A city boy, I spent the next two years of my life in an upstate orthopedic hospital that was surrounded by trees and fronted by the Hudson River. The New York State Reconstruction Home was the hospital's remarkably appropriate name. Two years later, when I returned to the streets in which I had grown up, I had been reconstructed only to the point where I could walk very haltingly on steel braces and crutches.

But polio had managed to teach me a number of other lessons as well. If it fed me a rich fantasy life, it also forced me to focus on survival. And it taught me that if I were to survive, I would have to become a man—and quickly. "Be a man!" my immigrant father would urge. I suspect that what he meant by that was, "Become an American. Do what you have to do to live." The year 1946 was a comparatively innocent time in this nation's psychological history. For better or worse, the country had very specific expectations of men. And of manhood. A man was expected to face adversity with courage, endurance, determination, and stoicism. With these, and with a touch of defiance, he might right the balance with his fate, however unjust and arbitrary that fate might appear.

"I couldn't take it, and I took it," says the wheelchair-doomed poolroom entrepreneur William Einhorn in Saul Bellow's *The Adventures of Augie March*. "And I can't take it, yet I do take it." I remember how thrilled I was when I first read those words in 1953. I was twenty years old by then. But I read them with the same shock of recognition Melville speaks of experiencing when he first read Hawthorne. I knew that Einhorn spoke for me, that he had given voice to the way I had learned to live my life and to make that life my own. And I knew that Einhorn spoke for scores of other men in this country who had confronted the legacy of a crippling disease or accident by risking whatever they possessed of substance in a nation that claimed to believe such risks were a man's wagers with his fate.

However unfashionable it may be to write this today, I use the word "men" intentionally. Like so much else in American life during the 1940s and 1950s, how one faced adversity was in part a question of gender. The memory of such cultural beliefs is embarrassing, but that embarrassment doesn't change the way our beliefs had been structured. Simply put, a woman endured, whereas a man fought back. You will get no argument from me if you label such thinking sexist. But I believed, and everyone I knew believed with me, that you were better off struggling with the effects of disease as a man than as a woman. Polio, for example, was a disease battled by being tough, aggressive, and decisive. And by assuming that all limitations could be overcome, beaten, conquered. In short, triumph over polio's effects lay in "being a man." One was expected to "beat" polio by outmuscling the disease.

By the time I was eighteen and had lived with the effects of polio for seven years, I felt I was a "better man" than my friends because I had managed to "overcome a handicap." And in the process of overcoming, I had shown that I could "take it." In the world inhabited by American men, to take it was a sign of being among the elect. Curiously enough, that was an assumption my "normal" friends shared. "You, you're lucky," my closest friend said to me during an intensely painful crisis in his own life. "You had polio." Strange to say, he meant it. And I believed it, too.

Obviously, though, I wasn't lucky. By the age of nineteen, I was already beginning to understand that no one ever "conquers" disease and no one ever "overcomes" its legacy. And yet I managed to look upon resistance to what my virus had made of me as the very essence of who I was as a person. I had reduced questions of manhood to a simple—I am tempted to write "simplistic"—syllogism: A man stands his ground, because not to do so is to reduce his presence. I insisted on self-reliance. No doubt I was structuring my life around what psychologists used to call overcompensation. But I believed that I could create my own possibilities from the very limitations of my crippled body. And so I walked mile after mile on my braces and crutches. I did hundreds of push-ups every day to build up my arms, shoulders, and chest. At night I would walk up the hill to the deserted children's playground in the dredged reservoir that the WPA had turned into the neighborhood's magnificent recreation area. Alone, I would do dips on the monkey bars for hours to create triceps strong enough to carry me endlessly through the days and nights of my need. At home, I would work out to the point of collapse, lying exhausted but pleased with my performance on the linoleum-covered floor of my bedroom in the Bronx. And through it all, my desire to create a "normal" life for myself—whatever I might have had in mind by "normal"—was strengthened into a curious insistence on meeting the virus on its own terms. I would become the man my disease had decreed I should be. I would take whatever it offered, and in taking it I would teach myself to draw strength from whatever it might do to me. If disease was a liability, it was also, I discovered, a gesture of promise. Long before I read Emerson, I knew a good deal about his doctrine of compensation.

I enlisted a hungry imagination in my service, and I took my heroes where I found them. A strange, disparate company of men were always at my call: Hemingway, whom I would write of years later as "my nurse" and whose tragic sense of loss seemed carved out of the continuing sense of absence the virus had insisted I live with; Pete Reiser, whom I had once dreamed of replacing in Ebbets Field's green pastures and whose remarkable penchant for crashing into outfield walls somehow fused in my mind with my own struggle against the virus; Franklin Delano Roosevelt, who had scornfully faced his own war with a virus with aristocratic disdain and patrician distance (years later, at a conference on the problems of the disabled in America, I would meet a historian who would disabuse me of that myth, a myth perpetuated, let me add, by almost all of Roosevelt's biographers); Henry Fonda and Gary Cooper, in whose resolute Anglo-Saxon faces Hollywood had blended the determination and strength and courage a man needed to survive as a man; and any number of boxers in whom heart, discipline, and training combined to stave off the defeats the body's limitations ultimately made inevitable.

These were the "manly" images I conjured up as I walked mile after mile through those quiet Bronx streets, as I relentlessly did series after series of dips on the deserted monkey bars in the children's playground at night, as I taught myself to go up and down one subway staircase after another by fantasizing that those concrete stairs were a collective insult thrust at me by the virus and that with each step I took I was crushing the virus beneath my crippled, brace-bound feet. Whatever else my life might have lacked, it certainly didn't lack focus. And they were still the "manly" images that flooded my mind when, fifteen years later, a Fulbright professor, married, the father of two boys of my own, I would muscle my brace-bound body onto a train in The Hague, grabbing hold of the vertical poles and swinging across the dead space between platform and carriage, filled with a self-congratulatory adolescent vanity as I watched amazement spread across the features of the Dutch train conductor.

Ambition needs to see itself reflected in the world. And resistance to fate is never abstract. It mirrors precisely those aspects of the emerging self we keep hidden from others but secretly cherish for ourselves. Time and time again, I had to remind myself of how men handled their diseases and their pain, or of how, at least, they were supposed to handle them. I realized even when I was in college that it was not the idea of manhood alone that had helped me fashion a life out of what the virus had done to me. I might think of Hemingway as "my nurse," but it had not been Hemingway but an immigrant Jewish mother—already transformed into a cliché by scores of male Jewish writers—who had serviced my crippled body's needs and who fed me—what I am embarrassed to write about even today—love and patience and care, while I fed her the rhetoric of my adolescent rage and "toughness."

Still, I did take it. And it was ultimately the need to prove myself an American man, tough, resilient, independent, and able to take it, that pulled me through my war with the virus. I have been, as every American man of my generation has been, reminded again and again of the price exacted for such ideas about manhood. At this point, I am quite willing to admit that my two sons will probably be better off in a country in which "manhood" will mean little more than, say, a name for an after-shave lotion. It has been more than forty years since my war with the virus began. Mortality creates its own bargains. And it is evident even to me that if mortality is the only legacy, defeat is the only guarantee. At fifty-one, my legs are still encased in braces and crutches are still cradled beneath my shoulders. My elbows are increasingly arthritic from the burden of all those streets walked and weights lifted and dips dipped and stairs climbed. My shoulders now burn with pain when I even remember the dips and the push-ups that would bring me vengeance upon my virus. And pain is no longer a source of resistance. It merely bores—and hurts.

But I remain an American man. If I know where I'm going, I know even better precisely where I've been. Best of all, I know the price I have paid for being there. A man endures the disease that has shaped him, until he one day recognizes in it the source of his vanity. He can't take it, but he takes it. There was a time when I relished my ability to take it. I'm tired of that now. And I find myself wishing that taking it were easier. In such quiet surrenders do we American men call it quits with the diseases that have shaped us.

Claiming the self

The cripple as American man

I am not a physician; I am not a psychologist; I am not a sociologist; indeed, I do not work in any aspect of health care. But I am a man who has lived all but eleven of his years here on earth as a cripple, a word I prefer to the euphemistic "handicapped" or "disabled," each of which does little more than further society's illusions about illness and accident and the effects of illness and accident. For to be "disabled" or "handicapped" is to deny oneself the rage, anger, and pride of having managed to survive as a cripple in America. If I know nothing else, I know that I have endured—and I know the price I have paid for that endurance.

As a writer and as a teacher of literature, I believe that the essence of what we like to call the human condition is each individual's struggle to claim a self, to create an *I* stamped with his own distinct individuality. This affirmation of the self is what we seek in biography and autobiography. It may exist beyond our capacity to create it, beyond our habits and virtues and will—but not beyond our need. I have never met a man or woman who did not want to stake a claim to an identifiable *I*.

Of course, it is a tentative claim, existing within the confines of a world in which we are never truly at home. Our capacities as individuals are always being tested. Everywhere we go, we seek to affirm the separate self, the identifiable *I* who possesses the strength and courage to withstand whatever tests lie in wait. Although it may be immodest to state it openly, the truth is that no one has a greater right to claim that *I* than a man who has wrested his sense of a separate identity from the very condition that threatened to declare his life as a man at an end. And however self-conscious and embarrassed I am about saying it, no one has a better right to claim that his sense of himself as a man has been seized from adversity than the cripple does.

Cripples are forced to affirm their existence and claim selfhood by pushing beyond those structures and categories their condition has created. On one level, this is what all men and women try to do. But in a culture that places such importance on the physical—however uncomfortable it may be with the actual body—the cripple's insistence on getting beyond the restrictions imposed by physical limitations is the kind of violent joining together of forces pulling in opposite directions that is characteristic of modern life.

It would be the most absurd nonsense to suggest that the cripple is envied by other Americans seeking to claim the *I*. No one *wants* to find himself the victim of disease or accident—no one, at least, who is rational. Anyone contemplating the prospect of spending the rest of his life in a wheelchair would exchange that fate for a normal pair of legs without a moment's hesitation. Ask me to give up the most visible symbols of being a cripple—in my case, the braces and crutches on which I walk—and I will jump at the chance. To insist on our capacity, to be willing to face the everyday risks that a cripple must confront simply to meet the world, to enjoy the sense of triumph that an *earned* mobility bestows—we can accept all this and yet hunger after what we lack. We can believe in our capacity to face whatever has to be faced; we can assume that we have paid a price for the existence we claim that others might not have been able to pay; we can think of ourselves as having confronted our fate even with such grandiose metaphors as Jacob wrestling with his angel. The one thing cripples cannot afford to do is to assume the luxury of lying to themselves.

Cripples are second-class citizens only because they are conscious of nothing so much as of the barriers the outside world places in their way. My hungers are invariably personal; the joys not tasted are joys not tasted *by me*. However simplistic my desires may seem to others, their significance is multiplied a thousand times by an imagination that knows what they are but has not been able to possess them. However absurd and childish they are as desires, I reach out and touch them in my imagination alone. And they are not abstract. They are available to any of those the distinguished social psychologist Erving Goffman labeled the "normals." That *they* should be able to touch them so easily, so unconsciously, infuriates me. For my life as a cripple tells me that a man should earn the self he claims. However successful I may be in the eyes of the world—and I certainly am, to use a phrase that should be burned out of the vocabulary, a man who has "overcome his handicap"—I am always measuring what I have against what I want. How do I tell the normals that I still dream about being able to run on the beach with my young sons (both of them long since grown adults), that I sometimes lie awake at night thinking about swinging a baseball bat again, that even as I visualize what I would do were I suddenly given the legs of a normal I know that what I want to do would seem stupid and banal in his normal eyes? I want to kick a football, jump rope, ride a bike, climb a mountain—not a mountain as metaphor but a real honest-to-god mountain—ride a horse. I want to make love differently; I want to drive differently; I want to know my sons differently. In short, I want to know the world as the normal is privileged to know it.

These are not great feats, not even for the imagination to conjure up. They do not call for special skills or training. But they are what *I* want—what I have never tasted or else tasted so long ago that the memories have become one with the desire, locked in a permanent embrace. And such memories frame all that is absent from my life.

People struggle not only to define themselves but to avoid being defined by others. But to be a cripple is to learn that one can be defined from outside. Our complaint against society is not that it ignores our presence but that it ignores our reality, our sense of ourselves as humans brave enough to capture our destinies against odds that are formidable. Here is where the cripple and society war with each other. If we were satisfied to be held up for compassion, to be infantilized on telethons, we would discover that this America has a great deal of time for us, a great deal of room for us in a heart open to praise for its own generosity. We are not, like Ellison's black man, invisible in America. But the outline of the shadow we cast has been created not by us but by those who will find a way to see what they want to see rather than what is there. In what we call literature, as well as in popular culture, we are what others make of us. In literature as demonic as Shakespeare's Richard III or as wooden as Lawrence's Clifford Chatterley, on television as bathetic as the stream of smiling children paraded before our eyes as if their palsy were Jerry Lewis's reason for living, what we invariably discover is that our true selves, our own inner lives, have been auctioned off so that we can be palatable rather than real. We can serve the world as victim or demon, the object of its charity or its terror. But the only thing we can be certain of is that the world would prefer to turn a blind eye and a deaf ear to our real selves—and that it will do precisely that until we impose those selves on the world.

Years ago, this recognition led me to write an essay entitled "Uncle Tom and Tiny Tim: Some Reflections on the Cripple as Negro." But the situation of the cripple in American society today seems to me considerably less grim than I described it in 1969. Tiny Tim is not the only image the cripple calls forth. The self wrested from adversity is a far more attractive image to be offered to society and ourselves.

And yet, society is more than a bit dubious about that image's validity. For if it honors what it sees as our suffering, it retreats before our need to define our inner lives, to speak of who and what we are. Society continues to need the ability to define us if it is to be comfortable with us. In its own eyes, it is society that defines our authenticity. I remember that when I returned at the age of thirteen from a two-year rehabilitation stay in a state home, my mother was immediately asked by the neighborhood chairman of the March of Dimes campaign (this was in 1946, before the introduction of the Salk vaccine) to go from door to door to collect in the campaign's annual fund drive. It seemed somehow natural: My mother possessed a kind of subaltern authenticity, for she was the mother of a cripple. Her presence at the door was supposed to remind our normal neighbors that their charity had been *earned*. Any other individual going from door to door would not have seemed as believable.

And the truth is that my mother *was* more effective, for she, along with our neighbors, assumed her authenticity. For the next forty years, long after the disease that had crippled me had been wiped out as a threat by the development of the Salk and Sabin vaccines, my mother made her annual door-to-door pilgrimage for the March of Dimes. Her "success" as a collector of charity was directly attributable to the sense our neighbors had that she was "the genuine article." Indeed, the kind of fund-raising she was doing mixes the comic and the bathetic, and it remains characteristic of efforts of such groups as the Shriners to support hospitals. The Shriners sponsor an annual all-star college football game that displays the salable talents of college athletes while giving everyone—sponsors, hospital executives, fans, professional football scouts, and players—a substantial charity fix. "Let strong legs run so that weak legs can walk" is the game's slogan. I can think of no better illustration of how society defines cripples as their condition. And it does this through the simple strategy of remaining purposely oblivious to the feelings it inspires in them. A child who thinks of himself or herself as an object for the charity of others has been defined as dependent. Only a considerable act of defiance can possibly save that child from the fate of being permanently dependent. In January, 1968, vacationing in Florida with my wife and two small children, I drove past a large shopping center. Strung out in huge black letters against a white marquee was a sign: "Help Crippled Kids! See Stalin's Limousine! Donation: $ 1.00."

Now, this is the kind of material Nathanael West or Woody Allen might have done justice to, for it is genuinely funny, a most human denial of the human. But it is also a definition of cripples from outside, one that remains the most formidable obstacle in their path as they push toward defining the self. They want to realize all that they can make out of their situation. Society, in turn, wants them to make it feel good. Even the act of reaching out for a real self is a challenge to what society tells cripples is their proper due. Their task is not only to claim a self but also to refuse to allow their pain to be marketed. The authenticity they must insist on is one that each person alone can create—not the cripple's nurses, not the doctors, not the teachers, not the social workers. For no one knows what his existence costs him as he does. No one has lived with the intimacy of his fears as he has. And no one understands better that the self's reality can be taken from the self's resistance. Better if Stalin's limo were laughed out of existence. Better if "Jerry's kids" forced Jerry to understand the immense psychological destructiveness of his telethons. Better if hospitals were viewed as a right to be paid for, not by charity, but by a rational society.

Part of me still hungers to perform those banal tasks that define the normal for all of us. But another part of me—perhaps the braver part—insists that the mark of a man is to acknowledge that he has been formed by the very accidents that have made him what he is. Perhaps the task of those of us who are crippled is to face honestly what the normal can choose to ignore, to take a chance on a conscious existence pulled from the remnants of disease or accident. Our condition is intense, our isolation massive. Society views us as both pariah and victim. We are pitied, shunned, labeled, classified, analyzed, and categorized. We are packed in the spiritual ice of a sanitized society in the hope that we can somehow be dealt with in some even more sanitized society of the future. Society will *permit* us anything, except the right to be what we can become. And yet without that right we cannot extricate ourselves from the role of supplicants for society's largesse.

If society is uncomfortable with us, it is not uncomfortable with what it can do for us. That shopping center sign was created for the same audience at whose doors my mother knocked. Those Jerry Lewis telethons are responded to by men and women who believe they are deeply concerned with "Jerry's kids." Those well-meaning Shriners in their silly hats interviewed at halftime do not intend to tamper with the cripple's need to establish a self. Accident and disease bring out the charitable in other men. They also bring out the sanctimonious and self-righteous in other men. What cripples discover they share is not a physical condition—the differences among them are far more pronounced than the differences between white and black, Jew and Gentile, German and Italian—so much as it is the experience of having been categorized by the normal world. For the normals, we possess a collective presence. For if cripples prove themselves capable of defining their own lives, then what excuse can normals offer for their failure? If cripples break with the restrictions placed upon their existence and insist that they will be what they have earned the right to be, then where does that leave the normals?

I do not wish to suggest that anyone is "better" for having suffered disease or disability. Nonsense does not cease being nonsense when it is cloaked in metaphysics or theology. All I mean is that cripples have no choice but to attempt to establish the terms and the boundaries of their existence, and that they should recognize that in choosing to do this they are going to offend those normals who have an interest in cripples remaining what they want to perceive. Only by turning stigma into strength can cripples avoid the categorization the normal world insists on thrusting upon them. "This is where I am because here is where I have placed myself." Only through scrupulous self-scrutiny can we hold up the ragged ends of our own existence and insist that the normals match our honesty with their own. In a mendacious time, during which what it really takes to become an authentic self has been buried beneath one or another variation on doing one's own thing, the cripple who chooses to be honest can at least keep faith with his wound.

Having already witnessed the power of chance and accident, cripples know that if the reconciliation of their needs with the world's actualities can lead to maturity, it can also lead to madness and despair and even suicide. Under the best of circumstances, maturity is not permanent. But when its necessity is dictated by disease or accident it is not only temporary, it is also what one is condemned to live with. Indeed, it can be said of cripples that they are condemned to adulthood. Every step one takes, every breath one draws, every time one makes love, crosses a street, drives a car, one lives out the terms of the adult's argument with responsibility for the self. The image of what one was or could have been smashes against the reality of what one is. And if one has accepted the rules of the game, then the sin of pride beckons—pride in performance, pride in one's capacity.

For there is a point at which the living on an everyday basis with that internal enemy who, as Ernest Becker wrote, unremittingly "threatens danger" leads to a certain haughtiness, perhaps even to a barely concealed sense of superiority to normals who have not been called upon to prove their selfhood. Our dirty little secret is the pride we may feel in a performance designed to impose the self on the world. For someone who has matched his or her will against possible destruction, the normal's frame of reference can seem comic, even banal, in the rhetoric it employs and the strategies it assumes. One who lives his daily life on intimate terms with pain can only listen in amazement to a sportscaster praising the courage of an athlete earning a great deal of money on enduring his "aching" knees.

But it is always within the power of the normals to diminish the cripples' sense of their own reality. We are, after all, trapped by the accoutrements of our existence. An individual may choose to create an authentic self out of defiance of accident or disease, but he cannot remake the truth of his condition. It is what it is. No matter what demands he makes upon himself, dead legs do not run and blind eyes do not see. The cripple can make of his injury an acquisition; he can transform his handicap into a symbol of endurance; he can formulate his very existence as an act of defiance. But he cannot change what has happened to him. He must recognize that his life is to be different in its essentials from the life of the normal person. He has learned to look on stigmatization itself as something he has earned. He comes to recognize that he has truly been set apart.

The process of recognition has been beautifully voiced in a poem by Karl Shapiro. The poem is about a soldier's loss of his leg during the Second World War. At first the soldier struggles to accept the loss of part of his body. The soldier discovers that he must learn to adapt to life without the leg even as the life he possesses is transformed into an act of defiance of the loss.

> Later, as if deliberately, his fingers
> Begin to explore the stump. He learns
> shape
> That is comfortable and tucked in
> like a sock.
> This has a sense of humor, this can
> despise
> The finest surgical limb, the dignity
> of limping,
> The nonsense of wheelchairs. Now he
> smiles to the wall:
> The Amputation becomes an acquisition.

But the soldier in "The Leg" will ultimately discover that even such hard-won acquisitions can be taken away by the society that insists on defining who he is, a society that will remain intent on shrinking his reality by insisting on its right to define the limits of his space, the boundaries of his quest for a self. And the effort to live honestly will pinch his sense of his own courage and test his ability to live on his own terms. For what we remember remains embedded in what we are—and in what we once were.

Freezing flesh

If tolerance is the virtue of the untouched, then I can be excused for the instant skepticism I used to feel when confronted by speculation about cryogenics. Listening to friends or acquaintances off on some sci-fi binge about the possibilities of freezing the body and its diseases until medical science could make that body whole and young again inevitably left me feeling that I had been caught eavesdropping on the intimate details of a sordid love affair. Men earn their skepticism. And I am a man who has walked on double long-legged braces and aluminum crutches for the past forty-four years. Such a man is going to stand at a hard distance from supermarket checkout headlines. I used to wince as solidly respectable academic colleagues spoke longingly—their voices filled with a caressing intimacy they would ordinarily reserve for a trusted lover at three in the morning—about the possibility of freezing some damaged body until it could be offered health and rejuvenation in the sanitized future.

These are serious people I am speaking about. But even serious people believe, in the secret recesses of their imaginations, that miracle-workers are supposed to work miracles. Dead nerves, blind eyes, atrophied muscles, brittle bones: sealed in icebound composure, they await the healing discoveries of the millennial years to come. And bet on it. As sure as God made apples, the sanitized time will come. Faith in progress demands it.

Think of what it would be like, says an old friend as he challenges my skepticism, if a palsied finger or paralyzed shoulder could shed debility by being encased in some prosthetic cocoon until called back into life by the healing gods. Oh yes, I think, what a coming-out that would be! In a homogenized time of healing, nerves regenerate and muscles are kissed by butterflies of electricity until they spring back into life. Let the chemical ice crack, and limbs that are hundreds of years old emerge as fresh as the morning dew. Poets write odes to the parts of the body, not to the consciousness of mind or the far reaches of imagination. "Sing, goddess, the wrath of Achilles," is preempted by invocations to the cryogenic muse: "Sing, goddess, the uncurling of the once-arthritic finger."

Molded by the fantasies of our age, I would happily deliver myself to Dr. McCoy's magical ministrations on the nightly reruns of *Star Trek* I avidly watch. Those supermarket checkout headlines frame my desires, too: invisible Martians who cure insomnia, cancers melted by mysterious beams of light, the blind who see and the lame who walk because our aspirations have themselves been frozen in time and imagination.

My left arm was recently frozen, anesthetized into a nondeath's dying to prevent a further weakening of fingers and wrist. Along with thousands of other Americans, I suffer from a degenerative nerve condition known as carpal tunnel syndrome. The surgical procedure my orthopedist suggested for me was an ulna nerve decompression at the elbow. My ulna nerve was to be transposed, embedded behind layers of muscle and fat to prevent further damage. Not as common as a tonsillectomy, Dr. Green assured me, but not so rare as to call forth fear and trembling on my part.

Forty-four years of walking on braces and crutches had jangled my left arm enough that at night electric currents stabbed from the crook of the elbow to the tips of my fingers, riddling the dark not merely with pain but with the threat of further degeneration. Had I not lost that battle with the virus at the age of eleven, the condition might have been caused by playing too much tennis or working long hours at a computer or practicing arpeggios.

But I was neither tennis bum nor computer whiz nor concert pianist. I was a crutch-walker. And a crutch-walker's hands are his bread and butter. The strength of my hands carried me, gave me the ability to go from here to there. An aging Hollywood beauty might seek to be frozen so that her superb face might still be worshiped in the sanitized future. My vanity was less glamorous. I was in love with my hands. I had loved them since the age of twelve, when I first started to walk on braces and crutches and I first realized the magnitude of my debt to them. Years back, I had spent six weeks at the MacDowell Colony. A sculptor asked me to pose for a head she wanted to carve. My response was to thrust my hands, fingers spread wide for her inspection, in front of her face and urge her to forget my head—which was, after all, a head like any other—and cast instead these hands that had served me so faithfully. My hands had carried me through the world, and they asked nothing in return beyond the daily pounding they were forced to endure. By the time I was in my mid-twenties, I was a connoisseur of hands, investing their shape with metaphysical substance. Let others admire Goya's sublime faces or Vermeer's young girl wistfully gazing out the window. When I walked through museum galleries rich with the color and splendor of the world, my eyes automatically searched out how the artist had created hands.

But my hands had endured more than even they were capable of enduring. My left hand now threatened to succumb to the pounding the ulna nerve had taken for forty-four years. The tips of my fingers were numb; the currents of pain were more and more persistent. "It's grown weaker," said Dr. Green in September as he urged me to push his fingers away with my pinky.

And it had grown weaker. "Pull down vanity!" wrote mad Ezra. In college, my hands and fingers were so strong I thumb-wrestled for drinks. I rarely lost. But a man's vanity is reduced in proportion to the realities he cannot overcome. The prospect of losing even more strength was frightening enough to make me nod my acquiescence when Dr. Green suggested the time had come for surgery.

I had experienced surgery before. In 1980, a brace I had neglected to lock sent me sprawling against the edge of my bathtub and smashed the femur of my right leg. Two days later, a stainless steel pin was inserted to cement the broken bone. The operation was successful. But memories of turbulent dreams and of a disoriented emergence from anesthesia were still strong enough to make me insist on local anesthetic this time. I wasn't afraid of dying while under the knife, nor was I afraid of being fed too strong a dose of anesthesia. Such deaths were mere statistical blips, chance interruptions in the natural order of things. What frightened me was the thought that total anesthesia would again unleash the boilings of that turbulent, disoriented imagination. I didn't want that. I didn't want to discover that endurance had given way to nightmare.

My surgery was scheduled for 8:00 A.M. on Wednesday. At 7:00, I was wheeled on a stretcher into the pre-op room, where a young woman introduced herself as the anesthesiologist who was to prepare me for surgery. Like so many younger physicians, she was eager to explain not only what she was to do but how she planned to do it.

I wasn't particularly interested in how my arm was to be frozen. "As long as I'm conscious," I said, "I don't really care what you do." Fine, Dr. Moody agreed. But sometimes, in perhaps 10 percent of cases, a local anesthetic didn't take. In that case, I would have to be sedated fully. "It'll take with me," I said. And added, like Joe Namath before Super Bowl III, "I guarantee it."

Nor did I care whether the stuff of my arm's frozen numbing was injected beneath the armpit or in my neck, the choices Dr. Moody offered me. I simply wanted to remain conscious. Frozen into numbness or not, the parts of my body were mine. I was not the aging actress or the androgynous media elf terrified of the decay of flesh. "All men are mortal. Caius is a man." That *all* was comfort enough. What was good enough for Caius was good enough for me. There were worse fates, I knew, than standing as a soldier in the ranks.

Dr. Moody chose to inject me beneath the armpit. For her, an injection designed to permit transposition of the ulna nerve. For me, an entry into the deep freeze of frozen flesh and heightened perceptions. I could hear the voices of my physicians. And yet I suddenly felt enmeshed in a long white silence which magnified shadow and substance. All fears had been calmed, all expectations reduced to the simplest essentials. As I first began drifting in that white silence, it struck me that the dream was not so much that torn or aging flesh might be made whole again but that time itself could be reduced to this slow-motion heightening of perception. For the hour and fifteen minutes I lay on that operating table, I believed that the world could rid itself of disease and decay and death.

Overwhelmed and liberated, I felt compressed within the frozen boundaries of my deadened arm. But I also felt freed from the limitations of bodily mortality. Do not misunderstand. Even as I lay in that white silence, I felt no desire to live forever. Nor was I under the illusion that my body was now immortal. But the lidocaine and ranitidine that had been injected into my left arm had clarified possibility. Never had I been more conscious of my ability to affect my own future. I felt as if I could halve my soul at will—and then, if I wanted, halve the halves. I was the body on which the surgery was taking place, and the mind responsible for orchestrating that surgery, a ballet master dancing to his own choreography.

Throughout the operation, I remained the object of my own scrutiny. I lay on the operating table, listening to Dr. Green and the resident assisting him discuss what was to be done next. Caught up in the clarity of that time, I had no desire to question the procedure. And yet I felt as if my mind were secretly directing everything that was being done. My doctor's skill and competence was a given in my imagination. But I needed to bend it to my will.

A leather strap around my middle held me in place on the narrow operating table. The left arm had been propped on an auxiliary table. I could hear Dr. Green and the resident, but I could not see them. A blue sheet kept the frozen arm and the two surgeons from my sight. Curiously enough, that screen reinforced the sense of control that had seized me with the injection of the anesthetic. The parts of my body were separate from me and separate from one another. And they were mine to command.

I had never "done drugs," not even in the sixties when it was virtually de rigueur for a young college professor who wanted to keep up with student fashions. I suppose I assumed a certain self-righteous contempt toward those who did drugs, not merely because I was (and probably still am) more judgmental than I like to admit, but because a man who must condition himself, day in and day out, to live with the aftereffects of a crippling disease cannot afford free-floating, untempered illusions. A cripple needs control. And early on he learns that if living is not a serious business, life certainly is.

Like Adam in the Garden naming the animals God parades before him, I felt that I alone could determine what was finger and what was elbow. The parts of the body I could not see remained mine to confirm. If necessary, I could control even the battered arm propped behind the blue sheet. Reality was distant; my power to control reality close at hand. Memories of stoned friends contemplating a single pore of skin or a jagged fingernail suddenly made sense. In this white silence, sight itself was magnified.

With an ease born of ignorance, I could contemplate separating myself from the parts of my body. Now that I have been brought back into mundane sobriety, I find myself wondering whether it is the sense of control rather than the promise of eternal youth that the aging beauty and doe-eyed androgyne seek. Perhaps, in the past, talk of cryogenics had irritated me because it was a thinly veiled need for religion not brave enough to acknowledge itself as religion. In the white silence of that operating room, besieged by the methodical hum of voices, I learned to understand that one does not compartmentalize pain—not, certainly, with local anesthetic alone.

The lights glaring down from the ceiling impose reality. For Dr. Green, they illuminate the new resting place of the transposed ulna nerve. For me, they are a fiery reminder of the real world that is about to reclaim me. I will return to a world in which damage to the flesh is no more than damage to the flesh. I would like to hold on to this heightened perception. But I know I can't keep it long.

"Please don't move your hand!" Dr. Green commands. I can't move my hand, I want to protest. I am suspended in air, a Calder mobile gently brushed by shifts in temperature. So precise is the sensation of separation that the disconnected parts of my body command changes in the atmosphere. Changes to which my numbed left arm, propped like a heavy lead weight on the auxiliary table, responds with trickles of involuntary movement.

For the real hand is no longer mine to move. The hand, the shoulder, the fingers, the entire arm—all frozen into liberation. The parts of the body struggle with each other for independence. Strapped to the operating table, I conjure up a scene from a horror movie. The scene is vivid, enmeshed in possibility. A bloodied hand propels itself across a white landscape. The hand has been severed from its body, severed from accountability.

I would like to tell Dr. Green about the severed hand feeding its own savage propensities. But I am once again picked up by the white silence. It is weaker now. I have faith in Dr. Green. Faith in one's physician, I decide, is an act of religious significance. Do we choose our physicians or do they choose us? They do when the wound declares the man. Dr. Green knows me. He knows my hands, has treated them, has watched the damage progress. And is now behind the blue sheet screen, working to stem the loss of power.

I have never told him how vain I am about my hands. Anyway, this surgery is not for my vanity but for my need. Would it change things if I cried out, "I can't move the hand!" Ultimately, the hand will be unfrozen. A slip of pain will course through my body, a beat of life testifying to a mundane consciousness I am no longer certain I want.

Dr. Green emerges from behind the sheet. He smiles. The operation is over. Everything has been achieved. Order has been restored to the world. "I never heard of that kind of surgery hurting anyone," a neurologist friend told me when I telephoned to ask whether I should go through with the operation. "It can't hurt. It should help."

The anesthesiologist is also smiling. A stretcher-bearer arrives. I am unstrapped and then lifted from the narrow table onto a bed. The arm, still frozen, is escorted with me. It has been placed in a splint that runs from wrist to shoulder, swathed in layers of cotton batting and ace bandages. It is my arm. Or will be when it emerges from this long freeze, this temporary death that is a premonition of things to come. Drained of optimism, emptied of the exhilaration of the white silence, euphoria lifts from my soul the way fog suddenly lifts from the Golden Gate at twilight. The glaring lights diminish fantasy. They diminish me, too.

I am pushed into the recovery room. The cubicle is surrounded by a yellow plastic curtain. After my bed has been pushed into place, the plastic curtain is opened, the shield lifted. I can see and be seen. Like reality, the recovery room is empty of promises. I feel deceived. I want to isolate myself from the six or seven other post-op patients in the recovery room. Parts of their bodies have also been frozen into rejuvenation.

Propped like a balanced rock beside me, my arm is still separate from the rest of my body. It sleeps in isolation. The rest of me is not asleep. The parts of the body have been rejoined to one another. The heightened perception has disappeared, the white silence broken by the post-op depression pervading the room. "Thou hast nor youth nor age / But as it were an after-dinner sleep / Dreaming on both."

In the far corner, a woman screams. The scream is followed by a series of evenly spaced moans. The timing is meticulous. Every five seconds, a whistle of air thrusts against the universe and a low moan emanates from the depths of her difficult dying. I do not want to look at the woman. But I look. She lies in the corner, moaning, as oblivious to the nurses and doctors gathered at the foot of her bed as they pretend to be to her. One moans in a specific language, I remember. As she lay dying, my grandmother moaned in Polish and Yiddish. When my mother's turn came, she moaned only in Yiddish. This woman moans in a language that I decide is some offshoot of Spanish. Maybe Portuguese. That she moans in Portuguese pleases me. She is old, in her late seventies or perhaps eighties. She is not big but she is all mass, a body shoveled onto a bed. The groans pace her rhythms, the way a metronome's ticking paces a musician at practice.

I turn my attention back to my hand. I cannot feel it yet. I am afraid I am going to break down, to weep myself into the boundaries of childhood. This is the other side of the white silence, this fearsome absence I had not bargained for. Why can't I feel my fingers? I stare at my hand. The fingers curled down, drooping like parched petals waiting for rain. My left arm—fingers, wrist, forearm, elbow—is paralyzed, dead, threatening never to awaken. I can feel nothing in the arm. I try to concentrate ownership on the dead hand. I probe it with the fingers of my right hand. I try to trace the tips of freezing. Nothing. No sensation. What is it going to be like to live with my two legs and my left arm paralyzed? If one is a quadriplegic when one loses the use of all his limbs, then losing the use of one's two legs and left arm make one . . . what? A triplegic. The word is funny, even in the mind.

Time drifts. I wish I could sleep. But I remain awake. The rhythm of the old woman's moaning is a tidal sound—in and out, in and out. I summon all the powers of concentration I possess and try once again to move the fingers of my left hand. Nothing. I can feel myself flushed and sweating from the exertion of will.

As if she had read my mind, Dr. Moody stands by my bed. The dead hand is the work of her freezing. I cannot feel the touch of her fingers on the hand. But I see her. I feel feverish, anxiety-ridden, flushed with cowardice. I struggle to keep myself from crying. "I can't feel anything. Not a thing."

"It'll be all right," Dr. Moody assures me, as if she were soothing a fearful child. "In a few hours. I promise."

"I can't feel a thing." My voice is subdued, but I think I am loudly crying out. "Don't you understand? Nothing."

"It will be all right," Dr. Moody repeats. "I promise."

And, of course, it is all right. At noon, when I am wheeled out of the recovery room, I can feel the tips of my fingers begin to unfreeze. A slow warmth, like a meandering brook, slips through the ice-locked arm. Terror evaporates as I focus on the slight movement I feel in the fingers. I concentrate on raising the hand at the wrist. If I can move the wrist, however slightly, I will free myself of the prospect of permanent paralysis. I close my eyes. I concentrate. And I remember. After the virus had taken my legs, I went for physical therapy sessions every day. The young physical therapist would run her fingers across the joining of thigh and trunk. She would bend down over me, urging me to concentrate on forcing the dead muscle back into life through the strength of my boy's will.

A confusion of needs then. Trying to will my dead legs back into life while fighting the sexual stirrings of those cool fingers tracing where the muscle should have been. Dreams of more than movement for an eleven-year-old boy. And now, forty-four years later, a middle-aged man serving as his own therapist, trying to will hand and arm back into life as the lidocaine and ranitidine wear off. The first intimations of postoperative pain flicker through the hand and wrist and elbow. The drooping fingers uncurl, washed by pain. This is not the sanitized future; this is the imperfect pain-ridden world of the here and now. And I am filled with a rush of gratitude to be part of it once again.

Affirmed by pain, my arm has come back to life. I cherish the dull ache that roots itself to the elbow. I hold a tuna fish sandwich, brought to me by a ward orderly, in the still numb but unfrozen fingers. I am, I realize, a happy man.

A few nights later, the left arm now propped between two pillows, I prepare for sleep. In my own bed, in my own room, staring up at my own ceiling. I frame the face of the still beautiful actress on the map of my need. The androgynous elf dances through the quiet air, aging away like the rest of us. I laugh. They are still seeking the freezing that will obliterate time. I can afford to laugh. Having emerged from my own brief freezing, I find myself wishing them well. And as I begin to feel myself drift off to a more common sleep, my healing hand reaching upward from the brace of the two pillows, I join their frozen dream of the future, my hands, my vanity, forever young and forever strong.

Writing the unlived life

I admire few writers more than I admire Orwell. I still more or less share his politics; I still envy the clarity and simplicity of his style; and I still take as my model his rigorous intellectual honesty. Having written that, let me add that I am invariably filled with a sense of disbelief whenever I reread the following line in the essay "Why I Write," published some two years before his death in 1948: "Every line of serious work that I have written since 1936 has been written, directly or indirectly, *against* totalitarianism and *for* democratic socialism, as I understand it." The line overwhelms me. I simply don't believe Orwell. And I cannot understand why a man so uncompromisingly honest was not as suspicious of political purpose in a writer as he was of religious purpose.

I may believe that democratic socialism is still the most just and equitable way men have discovered of living together, but I certainly don't believe that I or any other writer I know writes *for* it. I don't write for that cause. Nor for any other. The fact is that I write out of a selfish desire to alter the truth of my life, a truth I still find unbearable. I write so that I can look at what happened in my life and measure it against what I believe—somewhere so deep inside me that it has burrowed into the hidden corners and uncharted depths of my entire existence—should have happened. For me, writing is an act of vengeance, not an act of persuasion. I believe it is an act of vengeance for many writers in this country, each of them intent on reconstructing the imagination's record and setting it straight.

Few writers approach their craft in a spirit of altruism; few aspire, like Orwell, to making "political writing into an art"; few believe that their work will make the world a better or safer place; and few would claim, at least while sober, that the work they do will make a substantive difference in the lives of their readers. Writing as vengeance can make one selfish, even obsessive. But it is far more likely to send a man or woman to the typewriter than is the desire to change the world.

I am not a well-known writer. And at the age of fifty-three, I suspect I never shall be. But I have managed to write six books and edit some five or six others. I have also written more reviews and stories and essays than I care to count. I have done autobiography, fiction, essays, literary criticism, journalism. And with each word I wrote, I was searching for the boy who existed until I was eleven, when, as I melodramatically phrased it in my first book, *The Long Walk Home*, "the knife of virus severed legs from will and I found myself flat on my back, paralyzed with polio." But that virus gave me a writer's voice. For it was that virus which taught me how to see and what to look for. And it was that virus which forced me to recognize that in writing about who I was and how I lived, I was still speaking for that eleven-year-old boy, the *who* I should have been and the *how* I might have lived.

The Spanish Civil War, Orwell tells us, was the event that made him into a political writer. It certainly made him a better writer, more purposeful, able to command the material he pulled from a world he was intent on changing. Orwell hated the suffering of the English working class. I was more parochial. I hated my own suffering. I knew I would become a writer even as I lay with dead legs in a hospital reading and rereading John R. Tunis's *The Kid from Tomkinsville*, because I knew that only as a writer would I be able to visualize my life as it should have been as well as the way it was. Like Melville's Captain Ahab—whose acquaintance I had not yet made—I wanted vengeance on that which could have been either principle or accident but was in either case the cause of my loss. Let me grant at the outset that vengeance is a parochial motivation. But it is one I believe I share both with writers of Harlequin romances and with Nobel laureates. Is there a writer alive who does not need to re-create the unlived past?

Of course, at the age of eleven I didn't know what life had in store for me. But I already sensed that I would create and recreate both the self the virus had bequeathed me and the self it had robbed me of. I knew that as a writer I would have to conceive of the life not lived in order to understand the life lived. And I knew that in creating the man I was, I would have to come to terms with the man I had never been allowed to be. Even in writing a book review or a piece about, say, open admissions in the City University of New York, I would struggle with alternative lives. Within the writer who claimed his voice from dead legs lurked the remembered child, the runner still running. A writer chooses his own ghosts. That may be what is most attractive about his craft. And I was haunted, as I still am, by a sense of loss so constant it commanded every word. For me, writing was, is, and, I suspect, shall remain, "strictly personal."

The Long Walk Home was an autobiographical narrative, although a few of its reviewers thought it was a novel. The book opens as I am about to depart from the city for two weeks in a summer camp and it ends ten years later, as I am about to graduate from college and enter the world, convinced that "my war with the virus was over." About a year and a half after the book was published, I broke my wrist. Now, a broken wrist is not a particularly serious accident for most people, but for a man who walked on braces and crutches it was serious enough to send me back into the wheelchair I had left some twenty years earlier, when, properly rehabilitated, I returned from a hospital ward to my home in the Bronx. As I sat in my wheelchair at the age of thirty-three, nursing my broken wrist and thinking about what I would write next, I came to understand that my war with the virus would never be over. For the virus had created me. The virus had been transformed into the mote in the writer's eye. In taking my legs it had given me a way of looking at the world and at myself. Nothing I would ever write would be free of its legacy. What Chicago had been to Farrell, what war had been to Hemingway, what tradition had been to Eliot, my virus would be to me. I now understood that my virus (I'm surprised that I never gave it a name, for I certainly gave it a sex, male, and an identity, harsh, and a sense of humor, ironic and distant and playful) would stimulate and irritate me for the rest of my life. It was as if the virus had been reincarnated into a crotchety but interesting uncle, periodically popping up from some foreign land to probe my strengths and weaknesses and to teach me how to see. Like me, it had decided that the arrangement between us was to be "strictly personal."

I had originally worked on *The Long Walk Home* because I was convinced that I would never write anything else until I came to some kind of terms with what the virus had done to me. I remember having breakfast with my wife, one sunny morning after I had begun the book, and telling her that my purpose was to write a book free of the sentimentality and cant and papier-mâché religiosity usually found in such books. I was determined not to be inspirational. What I wanted to do, I explained, was to re-create the polio because it was the polio that had created me. The writers I had learned from—Farrell, Wright, Hemingway, Mailer, Dreiser—had all insisted that in order to see the world as it was, the writer had to look at it as if through a microscope. A narrow focus would force coherence onto a seemingly random series of events. My virus taught a different lesson. The body of the cripple was patched and blistered, and so was the story he would tell. Life was at one and the same time harsh and painful, tender and humorous.

A year or so before I began working on *The Long Walk Home*, James Agee's *Let Us Now Praise Famous Men* was reissued. Along with the Walker Evans photographs, which serve Agee's text as good lighting serves a painting, the book made a profound impression on me. In speaking of how he intended to deal with lives of such desperate courage, Agee wrote, "A piece of the body torn out by the roots might be more to the point." I still remember—and I am highly embarrassed by the memory—reading that line aloud to my wife. "That's my epigraph," I said. "That's what I want my book to do." Why I felt compelled to pull my body out by its roots—a rather horrible image, I now feel—and thrust my torn and bleeding carcass in front of some innocent reader is one of those mysteries writers learn to live with. But it seemed terribly important back in 1961.

The writer of autobiography constructs himself as a novelist constructs a character. But when one invents one's own self, a fairly strict balance sheet must be kept. In sitting down to write an autobiography at the tender age of twenty-seven, I understood that the glimpses of the past I would use would be selected by my virus. Almost everything prior to our meeting could be dismissed. Life for the writer began with the death of legs. Passion was rooted in absence and the desires absence evoked. Other than as a setting for the life the virus imposed on me, there seemed little worth writing about in the life of the child I had been. "I would sit by the bedroom window and think about that time before the polio," I wrote in the book's opening paragraph. "But it led nowhere. The only significance was the anonymity." My new man had been born. The life ended had called forth a new life, one that the writer in me would come to view as his "real life." At its heart, I saw myself as a kind of newborn infant, glowing with the expectation of knowing himself at his origins by looking back at the exact moment of his birth.

The novelist Richard Brickner also begins a book, his *My Second Twenty Years*, with the birth of his new self out of the death of the old. "In May of 1963, a few days after my twentieth birthday, I broke my neck in an automobile accident and lay for a while, precariously, on the furthest rim of existence." To live again as a paraplegic, Brickner depicts himself as a writer watching his beginning emerge from his ending. It is as if he is looking at himself, a surgeon preparing to demonstrate his skill before a room filled with students. He is the writer, and the writer's task is to dismiss his own past life so that his true "I," his new man, can step forward and take his place onstage. And it is the writer who controls the voice of that new man.

But the writer who discovers his voice in disease or accident makes a corollary discovery: he finds that he has become a victim of the reality he assumes. He may succeed in avoiding sentimentality, in treating his loss objectively. He may manage to control his tone, to speak matter-of-factly, as I tried to do in *The Long Walk Home*, or ironically, as Brickner does in *My Second Twenty Years*. But even as he manages this, he cannot escape his growing obsession with the self he was never allowed to possess. Every word he writes is an indictment of the life he was prevented from living. Possibilities impossible to realize line up in his imagination like demobbed soldiers, each waiting for its turn to speak for what might have happened in the unlived life.

And it is difficult to live with the intensity demanded by visions of the alternate life. The writer cannot, after all, permit himself to grow too involved with the life not lived. In real life, Melville's mad captain would have wound up behind a locked door, cared for by his young wife as she grew old, secretly mocked by his child. Too insistent a focus on what has been taken away can drive anyone beyond the edge. For me, a shield against that fate was the recognition that the virus was the reason why I wrote. In writing about what it had done to me, I discovered purpose as a writer. If I could put my sentences down, understanding that what had happened to me at eleven now stood at the heart of those sentences, then I somehow had reclaimed responsibility for my life from the virus. Let me admit that there is something just a bit crazy about this. And yet, just as a new life emerged out of the reality of dead legs, so the possibilities of the old life—the life not lived—formed themselves in my imagination as I traced what the virus had made of me. What had happened demanded the implicit recognition of what might have happened. The virus had become my eye. And it charted the growth of who I was while I longed to know who I might have been had the virus and I never met. I wrote *The Long Walk Home* because I sensed that unless I wrote it I could no longer live with what the virus had done to me. But in the process of writing I discovered that I had consciously condemned myself never to live without what it had done. An exchange had been made—the virus had my legs; I had its sight.

And for better or worse, its sight sentenced me to see everything—politics, sex, neighborhood bars, the subway, nuclear disarmament—through eyes it had bestowed on me. Some ten years after *The Long Walk Home* was published, I went back to the neighborhood in the Bronx where I had lived. It had been the kind of neighborhood that in the early 1970s was already being referred to as "a white ethnic enclave." And I intended to write a book about it.

All good writing, Hemingway was fond of saying, begins with a sense of geography. No doubt a good deal of bad writing begins with that same sense. Good or bad, it is not a literal geography but what his imagination lays claim to that concerns the writer. Boundaries dictate to life. But the primary geography lesson I learned while I was working on *Notes for the Two-Dollar Window* was that my virus had managed to fuse time and place so intricately that it was difficult to distinguish one from the other. To write of my neighborhood was to uncover the very source of my imagination, its shaping hand. And it was my virus that taught me that.

The way I looked at the world would not be changed simply because my focus was to be on my neighborhood rather than on me alone. For the virus, the self and its places proved indistinguishable. The streets I now examined were the same streets on which I had watched myself grow—first as the "normal" boy whose never-to-be coming-of-age would stand behind every word I wrote, then as the crippled adolescent and young man, finally as the writer returning to these streets to dredge memory and its meaning.

I was obviously one of the people *Notes* was about. Otherwise the book could not have been written. But the book's real protagonist is the Norwood neighborhood in the northeast Bronx, the rockstrewn lots that had not been filled in when the area was transformed in the late 1920s and early 1930s into the glint of gold in every real estate speculator's eye, the streets that had once buzzed with men and women and multitudes of children—Italian, Irish, Jewish—the parks and playgrounds and school yards marking off boundaries as intimate as they were familiar. Conglomerates of pain and ambition, hope and dread, these spoke of the neighborhood's story.

My original sense of the neighborhood had been formed when my family moved there in 1937. I was four then. Seven years later I had my meeting with the virus. I returned to the neighborhood from the hospital, remade and reconstructed, two years later, at the age of thirteen. I now walked with considerable difficulty, using double long-legged braces and crutches. But a more meaningful change for the writer I would become was that the neighborhood had also been reconstructed. From my new perspective, it was huge. The streets, the parks, the empty lots, the school yards—all had enlarged themselves during my two years in the hospital, all had leaped beyond the proportions of childhood. I would find myself struggling to take a few consecutive steps across avenues I had once run through. Or I would be standing on a street corner and catch the smell of my own past on the sudden rush of a summer breeze. Distance leaped beyond memory. The virus had destroyed my sense of proportion.

Even today, my memories of that period in my life challenge proportion. I see myself walking with my cousin in the school yard of P.S. 80. Once I could hit a ball from one end of that yard to the other. Now it would take me close to half an hour to walk the same distance the ball traveled in a second. And yet this seemed to me no more than part of the order the virus had given to my world. For a would-be writer, there was a certain excitement to it. The neighborhood was a bigger place. The world itself was bigger. Like Emerson, I had stumbled across the doctrine of compensation, a most valuable lesson for a writer. Change in the self dictated change in the world. For most children, distance shrinks; for me, it expanded. And if the world had become bigger, then it followed that the vision my virus gave me had become bigger too. The neighborhood had ballooned during the two years I'd spent in the hospital; it had burst its former boundaries apart. Was it any wonder, then, that my past life in it seemed a bit thin and dry? And is it any wonder that I would soon see that life as merely marking time before the virus?

In the 1970s I came back to the neighborhood as a visitor. And I came to it with conflicted selves, seemingly incapable of sharing memory. Each self, normal and cripple, projected its needs on the landscape. Each moved through a past populated by boys and girls, men and women, Gentile and Jew, all ghosts trying to root out what would be relevant to the writer. But those ghosts had their own wounds, less visible, perhaps, than the virus's other gift of braces and crutches but no less meaningful. And no less damaging or painful either. What is challenged in *Notes* is not the singularity of the virus's vision but the singularity of anyone's suffering. It was still the virus that was observing the world I saw. If the neighborhood reflected the pain and aspiration of *all* its inhabitants, both pain and aspiration were seen through the virus's insight.

A few pages from the book's end, I describe returning to the neighborhood with my friend Dominic, whom I have known since I was eight. We have come to eat dinner in a small Italian restaurant we used to frequent. But the restaurant has been transformed into one of those topless bars that sprang up like wild mushrooms in the forests of New York during the 1970s. Feeling as dingy as the now dingy streets, we walk away, across Mosholu Parkway, each of us attempting to assess his life. We are survivors. The imprint of my crutches on the grass of the parkway speaks of what the virus has done. But it is Dominic's sense of loss that anchors the passing of time—indeed, that anchors the passing of this "white ethnic enclave" we once called home. Dominic's life is a series of fragments that do not fit together. He feels betrayed by time. Survival for my friend Dominic has turned out to be more expensive than a mere encounter with a virus. The scars he carries are permanent, as deep, undoubtedly, as my own. At forty-three, he is still drifting through a life which, like our old neighborhood, has become its own dead end. His task is simply to get through each day. And he has no alternative conception of himself to fall back on—none, at least, that he voices to me. There are few other possibilities he can speak about. In *Notes* he is seen through the sight my virus has given me, not through his own eyes. A man who never really believed his life was his own to control, he has come home, searching for the drift's beginning.

We writers read the past through the lives we have lived, through the sight we have taken from those lives. Did the fact that I saw Dominic's life through the eyes given me by my virus make my sense of him any less compassionate? Would it have been better to use that life for a political statement? I don't know. But I often find myself wondering what Orwell would have made of the life of my friend Dominic. Of course, I have read Orwell on the harsh lives of the English working class; I have read *Down and Out in Paris and London*, *The Road to Wigan Pier*, and those splendid essays on England during the war. Still, I find myself wondering whether altruism is enough in our time. And much as I cherish Orwell, I also find myself more and more distrustful of any writer's desire to reform the world politically.

I no longer believe that a writer can hope to create political change—not in any significant sense, at least. For better or worse, my virus insisted that I see things differently. There was, I admit, a time I thought the day would come when I would discover I had written the virus out of me, when I would see clearly, the mote having been wiped away. That would be when the virus could be relegated, as Freud tells us *all* parents should be relegated, to that benign but skeptical indifference which remains the true imprimatur of the free man. Now I understand that such a time will never come. For no matter what I am writing, my virus is still with me, still the mote in my eye, still forcing me to look where I didn't plan to look and to see what I did not think I wanted to see. And the reason, finally, why I write. A simple revenge, at best.

The purpose of lifting

I began lifting weights in May, 1949, a few weeks before my sixteenth birthday. My closest friend and next-door neighbor, Frankie, had quit school—no one used the phrase "high school dropout" back then—to prepare himself for the Marine Corps. He had already enlisted, and he was bound for boot camp at Parris Island at the end of September. He had five months of life as a civilian in which to get his body into the shape the marines demanded.

Frankie bought a used York barbell set and then constructed a pressing bench from a slatted wooden cocktail table left unclaimed in the cellar of the Bronx apartment building in which we both lived. As a cripple, I was certainly not bound for the marines. But the door to Frankie's apartment was only a few feet from the door to our apartment. Curiously enough, losing the use of my legs to polio had served only to intensify the natural physical sense of oneself that preoccupies all adolescent boys. I might walk into Frankie's apartment on braces and crutches, but in my mind I saw myself as not only physically "normal" but the quintessence of health. And like any other male adolescent, I was already a sucker for anything that promised to test my strength and endurance. And so it was I found myself in Frankie's brightly lit room, lying on the cocktail table that had been thrust into service as a pressing bench, my brace-bound legs carefully straddling the bench, surrounded by steel bars, red-metal screw collars, and black cast-iron weights. On the light blue wall across from the converted cocktail table Frankie had taped a crayoned chart so that we could trace the growth of muscle and mass. The smell of our sweat mingled with the smells of cooking lasagna and baking apple pies that came from Frankie's mother's kitchen. An unexpected by-product of lifting was the sense I quickly had that even muscular power and definition were olfactory.

Assuming the role of mentor—he was, after all, a year older and had already invested himself with the proxy authority of the marine he would soon become—Frankie stood above me, urging me on, as I pressed one hundred pounds up and down, up and down. The strength surging through my shoulders and chest was electric, as much with anticipation as with performance. Frankie and I would take turns on the pressing bench, encouraging each other. Then we would sit opposite one another on two hardwood kitchen chairs, vigorously performing set after set of bicep curls.

Until Frankie left for the marines, our lives were structured by that bedroom gym. Both of us were conscious of the bodies we were remolding. Where we had once passed the time by speaking of the books we were reading or the ballplayers we admired or how the girls who filed out of the subway on the corner of 206th Street looked, we now talked about the geometry of muscularity, our conversation knowingly sprinkled with references to "lats" and "pecs" and "trapezius." The world of male adolescents has always been curiously hermetic and insular. Lifting weights fit it like a tight glove, serving to make it even more secretive.

More than anything else I did then, lifting existed beyond the boundaries established by my confrontation with the polio virus. When I first began lifting in Frankie's apartment, I told myself I was doing it to make walking on crutches easier by strengthening my arms and shoulders. But immediately after that first workout, I knew that lifting had as little to do with my need to build up strength in my arms in order to walk on the crutches as it did with Frankie's forthcoming life in the Marine Corps. The passion for working out, a passion each of us felt immediately, was shared by hundreds of thousands of young men throughout the country who were grunting and sweating as we were. All of us were lifting—no one called it "pumping iron" then—in hopes of molding our bodies into some Platonic vision of the ideal male form. Lifting was simply an act of male vanity. And we did it because we wanted to look good.

Of course, I wouldn't admit that in 1949. And neither would Frankie. I don't think anyone who lifted back in 1949 could admit to so flagrant a male vanity. The aspirations we might confess to were limited to bigger biceps, a firmer chest—and, of course, the admiration of the women we knew and the women we wanted to know.

There were other rationalizations for lifting, and at one time or another I probably used them all. I liked to tell myself, for instance, that my private ceremony endowed the world with order and proportion. As I grew older and began a doctorate in American studies, I would try to get myself to believe that by demanding effort, discipline, and patience of my body I was acting in pragmatic American fashion. I was making myself "better." Like the figure in the Charles Atlas ads in comic books I remembered from my childhood, I was making myself strong enough that no one could kick sand in my face.

As I grew less and less concerned with how I looked, I would find myself trying to break myself of the passion for working out with weights. Lifting, I now insisted in debates with an imaginary self, was narcissistic and self-indulgent. It was childish, an attempt to make the body into something greater than it was. And it lacked dignity. I was no longer an adolescent preening for others. I had become a husband, a father, a teacher. Orwell, Mann, Twain, Faulkner—I couldn't even imagine the writers I discussed with the students I taught sweating and straining beneath a burden so mundane as cast-iron weights. A man should learn to make do with the body he had been given. Or so, at least, I tried to convince myself.

But try as I might, I never fully succeeded in breaking the habit. Months would sometimes pass and I would refrain from lifting. And then a morning would arrive and I would suddenly find myself, like a reformed alcoholic trying to maintain his virtue as he stares at the window of a liquor store, staring at the dumbbells I kept stored beneath the bed. And on a day when the world threatened to overwhelm me, when it was simply too much with me, I would find myself seeking refuge in one or another gym laced with the vapors of sweat and Ben-Gay.

For a while, it was as if lifting alone promised to keep me sane. During the 1970s, I would flee the rhetorical excess that came to characterize the profession of college teaching for the very repetitive motions that I had tried to convince myself were senseless. The prospect of a good workout was sometimes the only thing enabling me to swim through that sea of words about "standards" and "relevance" we academics had unleashed upon ourselves and the nation.

It was also in the 1970s that I, along with others who had been weaned on free weights, began to use those high-tech machines with names such as Nautilus and Universal. The lush, carpeted spas of chrome and mirrors were a far cry from Frankie's bedroom with its makeshift pressing bench. But in one crucial respect the machines made the purpose of lifting clearer. In my mid-forties, strapped to the chrome and steel and vinyl of a Nautilus double chest machine, I finally came to accept the idea that lifting had little to do with any kind of vanity, either that of how I looked or that of how I performed. To strap oneself into these gleaming machines was to affirm the surety of habit, to remove the burden of time. It had nothing to do with the virus that had cut me down and it had nothing to do with an adolescent's hunger for a physical sense of his own body. It had to do, rather, not with what I had lost but with what I had gained—an ease of motion that, having been done, could be done over and over and over again. Repetition, concentration, endurance: it was with these I had to concern myself. And it was these that promised to carry me to the idea of a body stripped of any needs other than its own.

I still lift—light weights now. But still lifting. And I no longer need any other kind of justification when I feel the urge to do what I first began doing at the age of sixteen. I am neither looking better nor growing particularly stronger. And I have no burning desire to stay in shape. All I want is to lock myself into the sweetness of motion and repetition. I want to continue, one movement following another. How grateful one can become for doing just that.

La belle Américaine

A modern love story

In March, 1981, I hit the brakes as the light on the Avenue du Maine in Paris turned red. Four Frenchmen in their mid-twenties crossed in front of my car, a 1978 dark maroon Oldsmobile Delta 88, which I had shipped from New York to Le Havre. This was my first full day of driving in Paris, for I had picked my car up only the day before. One of the men paused to stare at the rocket emblem on the hood. Suddenly his face reddened, and the middle finger of his right hand pierced the gray Paris sky as he angrily cried out, "*Américaine*!" before hurrying off to rejoin his friends on the other side of the avenue.

I don't, to be honest, remember exactly what I cried out in retort as the light turned green and I gunned the Olds—probably the French equivalent of "And so's your mother!" I knew what had inspired the wrath of that young Frenchman crossing the avenue. It would have been bad enough if my country were under attack—but what had upset the young Frenchman was not my country so much as my car. For by 1981, my big American car had been identified as the enemy of automotive engineers and environmentalists alike. Never mind that it was also the lineal descendant of the car the French had made a very funny movie about twenty years earlier. Never mind that for me my car affirmed my right to master all roads in style and comfort. *La belle Américaine* was now the enemy.

I was an exchange professor that spring at a branch of the University of Paris unfashionable enough to be more or less reserved for African students, Arabs who had settled in France, housewives, working people, and assorted "others" considered less than properly French or academically sound. My driving destination that morning was an architectural monstrosity in the dreary working-class suburb of Saint-Denis where the university chose to offer lectures to those so academically unfashionable. When I pulled into the faculty parking lot, a pretty woman—one of the few middle-class Parisians among my students—leaned out of a second-story window, smiled, waved to me, then let drop a blob of spit intended for the same rocket emblem on the car's hood that had already infuriated the young man on the Avenue du Maine. After a lecture on the textual glories of Melville's *Moby Dick*, I suggested she explain to me why she had felt compelled to spit at my car. I would be driving the car in Paris for the next six months and I wanted to know precisely why it seemed so strong an object of contention. Nothing personal, she assured me. Her spitting on my car was an *action politique*, an act of vengeance for all the babies Oldsmobile had ostensibly napalmed in Vietnam. Then she frowned. Politics aside, she added, she felt it her duty to tell me that my car was too big, too powerful, too *Américaine* for the streets of Paris.

I had shipped my car to France because I walk on braces and crutches, the result of a childhood attack of polio that left me crippled. I need a car equipped with hand controls. And while hand controls were not entirely unknown in France in 1981, they were prohibitively expensive. To have installed them on a Peugeot 504, the smallest French-built car I could sit in comfortably, would have cost more than shipping my Olds from New York to Le Havre.

Economy was not the sole reason I would drive *la belle Américaine* through Paris for the next six months. By 1981, anyone who chose to drive such a car in Europe knew that he would be expected to pay a certain psychological price for the privilege. Big American cars were as unfashionable as a group of drunken furriers at an animal rights party hosted by Cleveland Amory. And yet, for an American who came of driving age during the 1950s and 1960s, driving precisely such a car was his birthright. And my personal passion for such cars remained fervent. I viewed the overpowered gas guzzler as among the gifts America had bestowed upon the world, along with Jefferson's belief in religious freedom, Whitman's poetry, baseball, William Faulkner's novels, and John Ford's westerns.

The Arab oil boycott of 1973 changed both the nation's driving habits and the nation's history. But for men like me, men who began driving between 1950 and 1972, a big, powerful car was a right of excess—a right available to all. Of course, even in the fifties I knew men who scorned the chrome portholes of the 1954 Buick Super—my first car, given me by my Uncle Morris in 1961. And even before the Arab oil embargo I knew men who insisted smaller was better and who mocked the tail fins that made the sixties Cadillac a steel-and-chrome leopard hungering to possess the open road. But such men could be dismissed as cranks or curmudgeons, themselves part of an American tradition. For me, nothing in the world was more functionally spacious than the trunk of that same Caddy. Americans talk a great deal about space. And I knew that a man going forth into the world could store all of life's necessities in that trunk, and a good deal of its luxuries, too. Space was ease, power—and space was as clear a definition of freedom as anyone might want. (I don't need Daniel Boone to remind me of that: Try placing a folding wheelchair, as I have been doing for the past six years, into what passes for a trunk in one of those squeezed, cut-down, underpowered, dehydrated glue-and-plastic machines we Americans call cars today.)

Like all great passions, mine for the big American car has mythicized itself. Oh, I still feel as passionately as ever about those oversized Oldses and Buicks and Caddies and Mercurys. And I continue to tell myself that a man who is six foot one and whose legs are encased in leather and steel has a God-given American right to spread out in the front seat of his car. But I also recognize that my love song to *la belle Américaine* will continue to be sung not for any pragmatic virtues the car possesses but because the beleaguered gas guzzler still embodies the democratization of possibility that an American of my generation associates with the open road. A man may not be what he drives, but he can be defined, in part at least, by the machine he chooses to get to where he is going. The truth is that my relationship to the American landscape, a landscape I continue to hunger after, was created by the big American car. It really is a big country. And what those oversized and overloaded machines promised was that a man could drive into the heart of his fantasies about America.

A curious love affair with a wrinkled and battered *grand dame*. Then again, those huge Oldsmobiles and Cadillacs and Buicks were never true luxury cars—not, at least, in the same sense that a Mercedes or a Rolls or a Jaguar can be called a luxury car. Stick a pink 1960s Caddy convertible on Route 66 in Oklahoma or New Mexico today and it will still absorb the landscape, taking into itself those boarded-up gas stations and shadowy reminders of what drove that road in earlier times. The big cars that almost overnight were transformed in 1973 into a collective Great Satan for environmentalists assumed power over the American landscape. No car can do that today. For the big car was itself a part of the landscape. And no one ever had to think of a finned sixties Caddy as an "investment," which is how I hear people speak about the prospective purchase of a Mercedes. What better gauge of our own diminution as a people? Isn't there something pitiful about a culture in which overpriced foreign cars and bubble gum cards with pictures of baseball players on them are viewed as "investments"? A big Caddy was not an investment, it was simply a machine meant to take you where you did not even know you wanted to go.

Throughout that spring and summer of 1981, my big Oldsmobile remained a visible affront to the Parisians. Before I shipped it back to New York in August, the rocket emblem on the hood had been stolen (I find myself hoping that it was copped not by my student La Pasionara or the angry young man crossing the Avenue du Maine but by one of those daring young Parisian motorcyclists who would be more at home among the myths and wreckage of Route 66 than most American men I know), my rear lights had been bashed in, my hubcaps had been removed one by one. *C'est la guerre.*

I like to think that what irritated the Parisians was not my big American car in itself. Paris was filled to bursting with Rolls Royces and Bentleys and stretched Mercedes limos that spring and summer. I like to think that what the French found irritating was the assumption of freedom the big American car had allowed generations of Americans to make. For such cars made driving a remarkably personal experience. Those tedious academic analyses of the big car as sex symbol or power symbol that were so popular during the 1960s were always off the mark. Most academics lack feeling for machines. Luddites of the imagination, they could not understand that our cars spoke not of sex or power but of liberation. And today's environmentalists who so self-righteously trumpet the demise of *la belle Américaine* simply do not understand the spontaneous freedom the big American car offered.

I know, of course, that my love affair is doomed. A few big-car models are still being built today, but the portholed Buick and finned Cadillac have gone the way of Henry Luce's American Century. In retrospect, an inevitable demise—and perhaps one even a lover should be grateful for. Still, I cannot help but feel that our early passions are our most fulfilling. To watch one's fresh-faced first love wrinkle is painful. And I cannot help recalling how those big cars gave me the privilege of knowing this country, of touching its geography. I remember the quiet romance of driving a powerful Oldsmobile north on Route 17 in North Carolina at five-thirty in the morning. I remember how the narrow January light had just begun to break the black of the sky. And I remember how it was as if my car had made me part of what I was driving through. It all seemed so clear, so natural—and, dare I mention it, so American.

And I remember driving a big, ugly gold 1971 Buick across the Texas Panhandle, the car's power and the horizon's depth making me feel I could drive forever into nowhere. And I remember driving with my ten-year-old son in that same big ugly Buick through the hauntingly lovely Manzano Mountains in New Mexico. We drove through small Chicano towns with tin-roofed churches, towns with names like Estancia and Tejique and Chillili.

We drove over a rut-pocked, half-paved side road until we found ourselves on a ridge overlooking the town pasture. We were lost. But we weren't really looking to be found. The pasture was, among other things, a Chicano automobile graveyard. Huge, rusted, overturned hulks and the small pickup trucks they dwarfed stood bleached and blistered beneath the midday sun. A few horses and sheep nibbled at the sparse grass between the dead cars. "It's like Stonehenge," Bruce said, recalling another drive we had made years ago. And it was—a Stonehenge where machines, like huge balanced rocks, fixed time with the death of function and froze memory itself to a landscape still hungrily awaiting the grace and power of *la belle Américaine*.

Invisible shadows

Self-reliance and authority

I feel about cities the way Thoreau felt about woods. When friends flee New York for some Arcadia complete with oversized houses and substantial plots of land, hundreds of miles away from the noise and congestion I need as my daily fix, I inevitably find myself taken by surprise. And although I dutifully make my pilgrimage to their rural paradise and gush about how fresh the air is and how green the view is and how splendid it is to grow one's own corn and squash and tomatoes, a day or two passes and I find myself mournfully sniffing the too-fresh air, hungering for some acrid reminder of man slashing against the beneficence of nature—any odor at all that will challenge the self-righteous assumptions about healthful living that capture the souls of those who leave the city for the country.

I confess these feelings hesitantly, for the truth is that, in the silence of my heart, my passion for cities seems to me as close to genuine perversity as our time allows. I am an indiscriminate lover of cities, *all* cities, and the prospect of visiting a new one or returning to one I have not seen in years makes me feel like a kid in a candy store.

That, in fact, was precisely the image that came to mind not long ago when my wife and I decided to divide our vacation time between two cities we knew and loved, San Francisco and Paris. But there was to be one change in our usual mode of touring: after forty years of walking on long-legged braces and crutches, my elbows and shoulders had announced they would no longer willingly endure those two- or three-mile walks to seek out some small, inexpensive restaurant a friend's friend had mentioned. Nor would they any longer accept the way I had mastered for edging my body sideways up a path—one so narrow it barely deserved the name "sidewalk"—on the slim chance that at its end I would discover some exquisite square.

I would be a wheelchair tourist now. And so, early one June morning, Harriet walking at my side, I found myself wheeling through the still-deserted corridors of Newark Airport, crutches strapped to the holder of my new aluminum wheelchair—the stamp of high-tech America gleaming from its lightweight, anodized body—as ostentatiously as an elephant gun strapped to the shoulder of a great white hunter on the Serengeti Plain. I wheeled inside the TWA 747, stood up, took my crutches, and nervously watched a stewardess fold the chair in half and store it inside a baggage compartment.

Edgy about the prospect of touring San Francisco in a wheelchair, I dozed off during the flight and dreamed of the city's steep hills. Ectoplasmic masks of Karl Malden and Michael Douglas in *The Streets of San Francisco* careened through my brittle sleep like the faces of two aging adolescents on the Coney Island Cyclone. I watched in horror as their police car hurtled out of control down the steep hills, siren screaming above the steady background drone of the jet engines. Then the car evaporated into my sleep, and in its place was my wheelchair—"You've bought the Jaguar of wheelchairs," boasted the salesman who sold it to me—hurtling down hills grown even steeper, an anodized streak crashing to a watery grave in the bay below. My body washed ashore on the rocks of Alcatraz—and I awoke, sweating.

I should have slept more securely. For behind its blend of styles, San Francisco is our true American claimant, a city with an unwavering sense of the practical. On the surface, no city should present greater difficulties for the wheelchair rider. San Francisco's hills are imposing, sometimes actually frightening, yet despite the famous hills, the city acknowledges people as what they make themselves. It applauds human self-sufficiency in ways that might have brought tears of joy to Emerson's unwatery New England eyes. Even its famed tolerance—the one virtue all its citizens, white, yellow, black, male, female, heterosexual, and homosexual, brag about—remains subservient to the city's remarkable appreciation of the pragmatic. San Francisco is the quintessential American city, more willing to take what it can use and better able to live with what strangers bring to it than New York or Chicago or Houston or Los Angeles or Philadelphia.

As a wheelchair rider, I found that San Francisco offered me the chance to exploit my condition. By making itself accessible the city challenged my sense of exploration. Rarely did I come across streets lacking wheelchair cuts, as I do constantly in my own New York (which despite its mayor's self-congratulatory bleating is more than ever a European city accidentally set down in the New World). Despite San Francisco's hills, the automobile there turned out to be a presence, not a dominant force. In San Francisco, to be in a wheelchair was simply to be in a wheelchair.

What choice did I have but to respond with generosity of spirit to a city that beckoned with such open and unabashed pragmatism? Even a New Yorker born and bred could learn to be a westerner, so each morning Harriet and I left our hotel near the rebuilt Cannery—now packaging tourists like us rather than Salinas Valley vegetables—for a two- or three-mile run through the city streets. Heading west across Jefferson, we reached the Municipal Pier. Like an eight-year-old testing the Rube Goldberg contraption he has built for the soapbox derby, I unleashed my Jaguar and raced, body bent low in the seat and arms pulling from as far back as I could bring them, to the end of the pier and back. Or else the two of us drifted east, against the flow of the country, moving through Fisherman's Wharf in its pre-tourist, early-morning stillness, then past the still-deserted docks into side streets that opened suddenly onto casual modern squares. Breakfasting on rolls and coffee, I relished the feel of my hands, touched the tender blisters that already promised calluses different from those of a crutch-walker. A different achievement harnessing the flesh. I wanted to laugh with delight. Breakfast over, my wife's feet and my wheels transported us at random, tourists glorying in the tour—to discover here a small bookstore selling off its last two copies of Charles Reznikoff's *Poems*, there a subtly garish drugstore boutique specializing in exotic multicolored soaps. Would not other cities, I reasoned joyously, be equally rich in possibility?

I do not mean that I pushed through those sunswept streets gratefully contemplating what Mayor Dianne Feinstein and her cohorts had done for those of us in wheelchairs. I, too, am an American, and like one of my early literary heroes, Augie March, I long ago decided to go at things freestyle; even a New York provincial quickly learns that the moment is his to exploit. But if possibilities abound, then San Francisco has made the prospect of seizing those possibilities less a war with society than a leap of self. It is a city which assumes adequacy in people, a city in which wheelchair cuts in the curbs are as natural as flowers in the parks or midmorning fog hanging across the Golden Gate, a city in which the right to explore the world is as important as the right to make money.

Touring San Francisco reinforced my belief that in America even affliction can be transformed into opportunity. Like an athlete or a ballet dancer, a wheelchair rider is constantly measuring his performance to see whether he has come up to standard, and he measures that performance against his own expectations. We Americans remain a people for whom the self exists outside even the limits the self imposes: aspiration is our true national religion. And on the streets of San Francisco, Emerson's legacy nestled in the heart of every hawker trying to sell me leather belts or windup dolls or silver balloons or "gen-yoo-whine Amer-Indian joolery." So essentially American a style invited me to transform pain into opportunity, to exploit my God-given right of self-dramatization —not the worst of sins in America, as both Walt Whitman and Norman Mailer instinctively understood.

My traveling days weren't over yet—not in my America, my rediscovered country. San Francisco had taught me that. For here I was, barreling down Leavenworth toward the bay at the bottom of the hill, toward that ultimate terror, as I had in my fretful sleep on the 747. Only now I could barely keep from shouting with the joy that shot through me. Of course, I felt embarrassed. I was fifty-two—not the age to remind oneself that an American is what an American does. I was long past the time when one should feel the splendor of plummeting like an arrow falling to earth, well beyond the age of exulting in possibility—even the risk of breaking one's neck at the bottom of the hill. At fifty-two no man should suddenly burn once again with the rebellious promise I now remembered feeling at the age of twelve, when I led an invasion of thirteen boys, all of us wheelchair residents in the New York State

Reconstruction Home (a name like the taste of ice cream in the mind), from West Haverstraw to the neighboring town of Garnerville, my imagination drunk on *Huckleberry Finn* and on the way Errol Flynn had died with his boots on in the weekly Friday night movie intended to take our minds off our "condition."

Does it make my joy less immature, more explainable, if I write that I was still taking my cue from childhood myths imposed on me by radio serials, pulp fiction, and the movies? Should I simply explain that what I was doing was moving west, admittedly in a wheelchair rather than a wagon train? Why explain at all? There are certain myths that Americans of my generation consider irrefutable. Geography reclaims the past. On San Francisco's hills, rolling into the wind springing from the bay, there was no need to claim maturity.

But for every west, there is an east. A month later, my wife and I flew to Paris.

If San Francisco had humanized a physical handicap, Paris magnified it into something thoroughly European. If San Francisco had insisted that a man could make do with who he was and what he had, Paris insisted that a man should learn to do without. If San Francisco had taught that a man could be strong enough and determined enough and, yes, brave enough to seize whatever possibilities might present themselves, Paris taught that a physical handicap violated the world's natural order, that it was close to original sin. The French, no longer a religious people, retain a profound respect for the forms of belief. They treat sinners as they treat children—first telling them what to do, then making it more or less impossible for them to do anything else.

But as I waited in front of the Air France check-in counter at Kennedy Airport that evening in late July, I was pleased with the prospect of the next few weeks. I knew Paris, had lived there four years earlier, and had been visiting on and off since the summer of 1960. And I remember how, when I left in August of 1981, the billboards had been plastered over with bright posters trumpeting the time as "the summer of the handicapped." Not that I could remember actually seeing any other handicapped people in Paris during the six months I had last lived there. In memory, the city had been amazingly devoid of cripples and their paraphernalia, like a De Chirico canvas in which everything human has been absorbed by shadows and angles and buildings. But friends who rode the Metro would tell me of signs reserving seats for those who had been wounded (as well as for pregnant women)—though few could remember ever actually seeing a man or woman in a wheelchair or on crutches in the Metro. But in the four years since I had last been there, perhaps Paris and *les handicappés* had grown used to each other.

Behind the counter, the agent for Air France smiled. "I will arrange to have you taken on board the plane," he said. "You can leave your wheelchair with me as baggage. You will be taken in one of our chairs." (Airlines customarily remove the outer rims from their wheelchairs, probably to prevent the chairs from being stolen: unfortunately, this makes it mandatory for the wheelchair rider to seek assistance, whether he ordinarily needs it or not.) But, I protested politely, I had taken my own wheelchair on board the TWA 747 to San Francisco a few weeks earlier. The agent, still smiling, shrugged. On Air France, he informed me, the "authorities" simply would not permit it. Why, I wanted to know, had the "authorities" on TWA permitted it? Another shrug. He could not speak for the American authorities—I suspect that, like Tocqueville, he instinctively understood how limited the power of authorities was in America—but on Air France, I simply had to be taken. *Sans* my wheelchair. *I* would not be taken, I responded—not by him, not by any attendant. Yet another shrug was his response. I stood up, took my crutches from their holder, and walked onto the 747. My wheelchair was taken.

Like Arab street sweepers and *plongeurs*, the handicapped in Paris fuse to what the French expect. They are conspicuous by absence. In two weeks, I did not see a single person on crutches, and I counted a total of only six wheelchairs—four holding children pushed by adults. On any single day in New York, within a half-mile of my apartment in Chelsea, I see more handicapped people pursuing their lives than I have seen in all the time I have spent in Paris.

And yet, however unfashionable such a confession may be at this time, the fact is that I love this city even more passionately than I love any other. And I genuinely like Parisians. Perhaps this was why I immediately found myself seeking excuses for their self-imposed blindness. Paris, I told myself, was a nineteenth-century city. Most of its streets were narrow. In Paris, the phrase "architectural barriers" called to mind hastily constructed barricades across the grand boulevards, behind which nervous troops stood ready to fire on a revolutionary populace. (I think of that splendid scene in Flaubert's *L'Education sentimentale*, when the policeman Sénécal betrays his revolutionary past and fires into the mob.)

But even as I made such excuses, I recognized that they lacked conviction. They were an American cripple's attempt to excuse in Europeans what he would never excuse in his compatriots. Actually, the problems the handicapped face in Paris, like the problems they face in the rest of Europe, have considerably less to do with architectural shortcomings than with European attitudes toward disease. Architectural barriers are problems in physical structure, and problems in structure have always been comparatively easy for Europeans to deal with. Cultural barriers, however, are problems of morphology, which deny the very ways a society wishes to see itself. The truth is that, in some peculiar way I still do not wholly understand, to be a cripple in Paris is to indict the French, who have perfected the art of not seeing what they do not wish to see.

I am speaking, of course, of basic attitudes toward handicap, not about social services, which are probably better in almost any Western European country than they are now in America. What I mean specifically is the sense of possibility available to someone who is crippled. In Europe, where the cripple is unconsciously but effectively kept out of sight because his presence somehow embodies those very imperfections fate has in store for all, such a sense is minimal. The cripple, transformed into an emblem of what others fear, is not "allowed" by the "authorities"—those same authorities who often are responsible for the social services he is allowed—to stake his claim to the kind of independence San Francisco accepts as his by right of being. His existence makes Europeans uncomfortable, and so he is "given" what he needs—except presence. In Europe, apparently, it is better to ignore an itch than to be seen scratching in public.

Like the movement for the rights of women, the movement for the rights of the handicapped is considerably stronger in the United States than it is in Europe. I suspect that the reasons for this are fairly traditional. Despite their rhetoric, such movements are not really political, or at least nor primarily political. They challenge not power but ideas of order and form, the very ideas so deeply ingrained in European consciousness. Respect for the "authorities" anchors European culture—even, peculiarly enough, among those who call themselves anarchists—and such respect goes unchallenged even by the intellectual left. (I sometimes find myself wondering whether this is what accounts for the number of people in Europe, particularly the number of intellectuals, who announce that they are anarchists and turn out to be those who deny authority under the aegis of the authorities.) I quickly discovered that, when I spoke of my problems to my Parisian friends on the left, I confronted neither understanding nor empathy. Were I speaking of my right to a pension, my right to adequate medical care, or my right to an adequate diet, I would have stood within the boundaries their experience circumscribed. But I was speaking about my right to cross a street and enter a museum. And I was, I learned, pushing against *their* ideas of order, *their* proprieties. In Europe, such fixed attitudes deny not the cripple's physical condition but his adulthood.

In France, as Sartre showed, words often fashion relationships beyond the necessity of action. And the word usually looms larger than the deed. On the morning after our arrival, Harriet and I set out for the Grand Palais, where Renoir was being given one of those periodic acts of homage the French are so fond of. The distance between our hotel on the boulevard Montparnasse and the Grand Palais was some six or seven kilometers. Despite the absence of wheelchair cuts in the curbs, we managed to improvise well enough that I found myself thinking Paris in a wheelchair might be as easy as San Francisco.

At the exhibit, however, I rediscovered the authorities—dressed now as museum guards. I also discovered that, whereas in American museums I was free to go where I wished, in the Grand Palais I would have to be escorted from one level of the exhibition to the next on a kind of electric platform connected to the staircase banister. There were *ascenseurs* in the Grand Palais, but for reasons never made clear they were not to be used by *les handicappés*. *We* had to be taken, escorted. Had I been "allowed" (how that word haunts one's imagination in Europe) to operate the electric platform myself, I would have found my situation irritating but tolerable. But I was *not* allowed. In Paris, people lived and died by rules of order—singular proprieties to be swallowed, as a child takes castor oil. At each change of level, the guard puffed with importance like a sail in a swell of wind. And at each change of level, I confronted a different guard, each an authority speaking for the authorities.

I watch as the guard presses the button I could so easily have pressed myself. As the chair slowly ascends the staircase, he walks at my side. He is an animal trainer and I am a trained lion. My sense of accomplishment at having maneuvered the streets of Paris evaporates. I have been transmogrified from independent American into European supplicant, Quasimodo robbed of his bells and tower. But I say nothing. I have been cowed.

The following day found us once again on the boulevard Montparnasse, moving toward the Hôtel Biron, where the Rodin Museum is housed. Two groups of masons were working on opposite sides of the street, cementing into place sloping curbs that had obviously been cut for wheelchair access. I pushed faster, my spirits restored, a rush of expectation feeding me energy.

"Be careful!" my wife warned. "Don't hope carelessly."

But I chose to hope—carelessly or not. By the time we reached the Hôtel Biron and I spotted the blue-and-white wheelchair-access sign, I felt euphoric. I raced ahead of Harriet, pushed straight up the metal ramp, and then suddenly halted in front of a single stone step. A guard stared down at me. I tried to speak, heard my French break into incoherent gesticulation. Why, I raged to myself, hadn't the ramp been run all the way up into the entrance? Why did I once again find myself at the mercy of the authorities? Why could not Paris, Europe, the whole of Western culture I had been brought up to worship, understand that what I wanted was responsibility for my own comings and goings? "Why," I hear myself furiously ask the uncomprehending guard in English, "can't Paris be like San Francisco?"

I stand. I remove the crutches from the holder. I mount the

step. The guard is still smiling. He lifts my wheelchair inside and brushes the seat with his hand. As I sit down, I envision murder.

When Harriet and I returned to our hotel a few hours later, the wheelchair cuts in the curbs had been cemented into place. The work had been finished. The masons had gone home, or perhaps to another job. In front of each curb cut, making it impossible for me to mount the sidewalk, stood a small parked car.

For the next two days I continued my attempt to tour Paris in a wheelchair. But I had already been defeated, and I knew it. I was now engaged in a cause divorced from aching shoulders and elbows. For the first time since I had started coming here some twenty-five years ago, the city seemed truly inhospitable. The few toilets that displayed the wheelchair-access sign were invariably built on stone floors so wet and slippery that they were an invitation to suicide; parks and streets were filled with dog droppings, even where signs insisted dogs were forbidden; in front of each sloping curb cut stood a parked car; to see a movie, I had to mount two or three flights of stairs; to get to a restaurant restroom, I had to walk up or down a curving flight of marble stairs. Word and deed embraced only in the imagination. The summer of the handicapped had long since ended.

For me, the lines had once again been drawn between Europe and the United States. San Francisco had signaled that even in a wheelchair a man might yet define his existence for himself. In contrast, Paris insisted that because a person was in a wheelchair he was expected to live his life *without*—without movies, without restaurants, without mobility, without adulthood, and above all, without the blessing of the authorities. Each city had delivered its message about what people were and were not entitled to do with their lives.

I do not intend to claim that we can derive a social ethic from how a culture looks at the handicapped. And yet, let me also note that the different ways cultures regard what Susan Sontag once called "a more onerous citizenship" must be granted significance, and that to examine those differences is to understand how attitudes toward handicap go beyond the immediate concerns of the handicapped themselves. Such differences speak, ultimately, of how men view themselves and of how they envision the good society. It is not the afflictions of men but their possibilities that remain at issue between Europe and America.

San Francisco, whatever its shortcomings, speaks in an American voice, while Paris still insists that form and substance are one and the same. Men speak of themselves when they address the problems of others, and for me, attitudes toward physical handicap illustrate why Hans Castorp must ultimately prove more beneficial to society than that good soldier, his cousin Joachim. San Francisco is no longer the wide-open frontier town celebrated by Mark Twain and Jack London, and Paris is no longer the highly stratified city of Proust and Zola. But the one remains American and the other remains European. In these United States, a country I have been arguing with all my life, people continue to believe in the primacy of their right to define themselves in spite of—one is tempted to write "in the face of"—what it is they have lost. In the final analysis, one creates one's own metaphors out of disease, and American metaphors are more moving, more attractive, than their European counterparts, if only because they admit the possibility of tension and struggle.

I am, I now know, going to spend the rest of my life in a wheelchair. I suspect that I am better off spending that life as a crippled American than as a crippled European. To some extent, invisibility remains the fate thrust on the handicapped by all cultures, but in the United States invisibility at least casts a shadow. San Francisco does not cripple the cripple's spirit. Paris does—because its sense of good and evil still derives from the language of the "authorities."

After four days of trying to battle the French insistence that I was what the authorities had chosen to make me, I folded my Jaguar of wheelchairs in half and stored it in the bathroom. For the next ten days, I ignored the protests of my shoulders and elbows and proceeded to fall in love all over again with a city whose greatest appeal is that it remains swollen with a singular sense of itself. On the rue d'Assass, Harriet and I stumbled across the house of the great sculptor Zadkine, now a small jewel of a museum; in the solemn spaces of the boulevard de Latour-Maubourg we were delighted to discover that dinner at our favorite restaurant was as good as ever (and in that summer of the inflated dollar, considerably cheaper than before); clouds skimmed the rooftops of Paris, and the rooftops of Paris still cried out for painters worthy of their angles.

It was still a rich, splendid city, but it had forced me to surrender my rights of exploration. Rich as it was, Paris was still European.

On the day before we are scheduled to fly back to New York, Harriet and I stand in the Cour de Mai watching an officious policeman direct Dutch and English and Japanese tourists to the Sainte-Chapelle. Harriet slips into a line waiting to go inside. I remain behind, leaning against an iron railing and bracing myself on my crutches. I stare up at the spire of Sainte-Chapelle. On this cool August morning, the spire thrusts into dark bands of clouds that seem to strike at it like spinning gray fists. Apprehensive, I force my eyes back to the cobblestones. Glancing left, I notice a concrete ramp leading down to a wide door with a blue-and-white wheelchair-access sign. Every guidebook I have ever read calls Sainte-Chapelle "a miracle in stone." What better place for a more modest miracle—one that will testify that Paris, too, has admitted the world people demand? I walk down the ramp on my crutches. I stand in front of the door. Silently, I reach out and grab the brass doorknob, as if I were shaking hands with a new friend.

I turn the knob. But the door is locked.

I make my way back up the concrete ramp. I am still on crutches, still an American, and—in this Europe—still invisible. Tomorrow, I remind myself, I will head west. Tomorrow I will be going home.

The wolf in the pit in the zoo

The cripple in American literature

One of the hits of the 1985 theater season in England was a new production of *Richard III* mounted by the Royal Shakespeare Company. Anthony Sher's Richard was hailed as one of the more memorable performances of a role that has always seemed to me the very embodiment of the rage and passion that stamp the existence of the cripple. A good friend of mine, who happens to be a noted Shakespearean scholar, was fortunate enough to see the performance at Stratford and described the play's opening to me. As the lights dim and the curtain goes up, the audience hears Sher, speaking quietly but firmly, establish Richard's presence. From the start, the audience is aware that Richard's is a crippled presence: "But I, that was not framed for sportive tricks." As Sher concludes "the winter of our discontent" soliloquy, he advances menacingly upon the audience, swinging on two wooden crutches that propel his body forward as if he were about to hurl himself on the viewers. My friend described Sher as bounding on the crutches like some intimidating animal moving across the stage. Throughout the performance, the crutches embodied Richard's formulation of himself, his menacing sense of injustice—both a prop for the actor and a weapon with which he flailed away at his audience's well-being.

My friend told me that during the course of the performance he came to view Sher's Richard as the quintessential cripple. Everything in the play could be traced back to Richard's consciousness of himself as a "deformed, unfinished" man. After the performance, my friend went backstage with some other Shakespeareans to ask Sher how he had arrived at his conception of Richard. And why the crutches? A year or so earlier, it turned out, Sher had snapped an Achilles tendon and had been forced to get around on crutches for about two months. As a result, he encountered that same sense of displacement and alienation that an individual who is permanently bound to his crutches encounters constantly. Casual passersby stared; he found himself the object of a naked, unabashed curiosity as depersonalized as it was indifferent to his sense of himself; and he felt growing within himself rage at how what he could and could not do was defined by others; he became increasingly irritable as well as impatient. At what specific point he seized on his own experience as a crutch-walker as the source of his characterization of Richard is not particularly important. What is important is that Sher had come to see Richard as an individual who was first cripple and then man. Sher recognized that Richard's relation to the world derived in large measure from the inadequacy of his body.

Act I concludes with Richard's coronation, after he has ruthlessly murdered all who stand in the way of his seizing the crown.

In the production at Stratford, Sher was carried before the throne in a sedan chair, the only time in the entire performance he is seen onstage without his crutches. Wearing a flowing red cape, he ascends stairs to the coronation throne, literally crawling up the steps with a hunger and rage that make him both threatening and helpless. Sher's body is filled with a "serpentine terror," and it transforms him as surely as the crutches do. In these two images—crutches used as weapons propel the crippled king across the stage even as they intimidate the audience, and the legless serpentine ascent of the stairs to make legitimate a crown for which he has schemed and murdered—Shakespeare has hit upon the two fundamental images that cripples are accorded in Western literature. The accoutrements on which the cripple is dependent, his crutches, are made into a weapon, almost a primal force, to threaten both Richard's subjects and the audience watching the crippled king impose his diabolical ambition on those subjects. But the red-caped, demonic figure crawls, like some giant insect or snake, up the stairs to take that of which he has cheated others. Imposing his limitations to rob legitimacy, Sher's broken, twisted body begs for compassion. There is little to be added to these two images from Western literature's view of the cripple, although there are any number of variations on the themes they suggest. The cripple is both demonic threat and pitiful recipient of compassion—to be damned, to be pitied, and frequently to be damned as he is pitied.

Images of disability have always been important in Western myth and literature. Probably all cultures link physical handicap to moral culpability. Stigmatization, one suspects, is prehistorical. Is there, for example, another god so blatantly used as the crippled god of the smiths, Hephaestus? The Greeks of the classical world saw the cripple as the man defined by others (Hephaestus) and the man defined by his own excess (Oedipus). They balanced the cripple as cuckold with the cripple who goes beyond the boundaries acceptable to the "normal."

Physical health and moral virtue are not synonymous in Western culture, but they are closely related. In American literature, one can argue that it is the body, not the mind, that declares moral primacy. Even today, when the traditional idea of manhood is under attack, the skills by which a man claims his space in America are surprisingly physical. It is his skill with rifle and tomahawk, not his Christian piety, that carries Natty Bumppo from the seeker we meet in *The Deerslayer* to the saintly figure who dies so splendidly in *The Prairie*. Even the idea of communion with other men, the brotherhood of the spirit, springs from a sound body and a clear spirit. When Whitman chants "the body electric," he first makes certain that his "perfect health" is known to all. Only a true child of the wilderness can sound his "barbaric yawp over the roofs of the world." Thoreau discovers the unfettered self everywhere a real man roams. Even Emerson declares the primacy of the physical, linking the strong body to the active mind long before Theodore Roosevelt sets out to teach his fellow Americans the virtues of the strenuous life. "We will walk on our own feet; we will work with our own hands; we will speak our own minds."

As it so frequently does, American culture loosens European strictures, while maintaining allegiance to the dominant Western cultural myths and the forms those myths are given. Only in a country where physical self-reliance was looked upon as a God-given right could a man as intelligent as Emerson view society as a "conspiracy against the manhood of every one of its members." However homoerotic their own sexuality appears to us today, the image of manhood bequeathed to us by the major writers of the American Renaissance (Hawthorne is the exception here) was that of physical health and manly vigor. The writer's obligation was to affirm the virtue of man in the wilderness—and that virtue was predominantly physical.

But not even the untamed wilderness could hide the nation's misfits. Incapable of meeting the physical challenge of the wilderness, the infirm of body discovered that the virtues the culture celebrated were not the virtues they possessed. If the wilderness allowed ordinary men the opportunity to be heroic, to confront their inner selves and external opportunity at one and the same time, what did it offer—even as an image—to the cripple? The physical skills the wilderness demanded as it offered itself for conquest were precisely those skills the cripple lacked. Tiny Tim cannot light out for the Territory as Huck Finn threatens to do. The cripple cannot exist outside the boundaries of a society upon which he is dependent. He cannot claim that he is dependent solely upon his own physical mastery of the universe.

American writers, by and large, have viewed the world from the vantage point of the "normals." They may like to think of themselves as rebels, but the rebellions more often than not reinforced American culture's idea of what is and is not desirable. What Philip Rahv called "the cult of experience" in American writing is rooted in our male writers' desire to prove themselves as "manly" as the culture to which they speak. By the same token, most writers look at the cripple and the visible stigmatization he bears with the same suspicion and distaste found in the rest of the culture. The images that exist in literature exist only because the need for those images exists in life. The landscape inhabited by the cripple is strange and shadowy, and it is held up to judgment by those who live in fear of it.

In America, as in the rest of Western culture, illness of any kind is a state begging to be interpreted. And interpretation invariably embraces judgment. One can create a sense of virtue even through one's ability to avoid accident or disease. "There but for the grace of God go I" can so easily be transformed into "There through the judgment of God goes he."

Where health is a virtue, disease is at least an insufficiency, if it is not a vice. Even if one argues, as I have, that it is possible to create our own metaphors from disease or accident—images that sustain our determination to resist the fate society may deem properly ours—these personal images must still battle against the extraordinary power of the cultural metaphors imposed from outside. It is the social dimension of disease and disability that is depicted in popular images. For generations, blacks were asked to see their lives in the comic obsequiousness of Butterfly McQueen and Stepin Fetchit. An image can become so pervasive that its consequences are swallowed up by the welter of moralistic judgments it calls forth.

In life, this view of disease as the manifestation of judgment can take many forms. But in literature, the effect is broader by being made narrower. How often is it argued, for instance, that Lawrence's Clifford Chatterley is the end product of a literary imagination that belonged to a moralistic bully? Even those who condemn Lawrence for his sexism usually brush over Clifford Chatterley lightly. As impotent and mechanical as the wheelchair to which he is bound, Clifford Chatterley's appearance as the crippled industrialist has behind it a good many of the taboos of Western culture. In Lawrence's eyes, Chatterley is crippled because both he and Western man—for whom he stands as representative—have lost courage. His wound embodies that moral equation by means of which the victim pays double for his victimization, rather like Ezra Pound accusing the Jews of leading the Gentiles to slaughter during the Second World War. Lawrence expects his readers to stand up and cheer as his runty little gamekeeper awakens Lady Constance to the joys and tremors of the real woman within. In the novel, the cripple's wound presents his wife with the opportunity to liberate her sexuality by making him a cuckold. Never mind what it does to the cripple himself.

Of course, Lawrence was a genius, and in a story such as "The Blind Man" he managed to create one of the more intriguing portraits of disability in English literature, endowing the sightless Maurice Pervin, another victim of modern warfare, with the kind of physical magnetism that makes him as sexual as Chatterley is impotent. This has proven more difficult to do in American literature, where disease and mortality have been linked by a formidable theological underpinning. Mutability permeated early American culture, as the historian David Stannard has pointed out in *The Puritan Way of Death*. In many ways, a consuming concentration on death makes the cripple less marginal to society. Where men and women were exhorted to "keep their eyes on a heavenly goal," there was neither the time nor the inclination to question disease and its effects. Disease contributed to that powerful sense of ending characteristic of Protestant societies. Not until the nineteenth century did images of the physical cripple—the lame, the halt, the blind—take on their modern connotations in American literature.

One can speak of the modern view of the cripple in literature when the character and his stigmatization are merged. It is only when the cripple's character is the direct result of his stigmatization that his physical condition becomes the source rather than the symbol of his fate. It is then that he discovers it is not his disease that evokes a sense of wonder in others but the judgments his disease calls forth. Doomed to remain outside the experience of those who watch his every move through the eye of their judgment, he incorporates in his life the fears and superstitions of the society that measures him. Piety and demonism mix in his life. His disability, he learns, is not his true problem: His greatest handicap is not the accident or disease that has crippled him but what society has made of that accident or disease. And because self-reliance must be a physical possibility before it can be made into anything else, images of his incapacity battle against images of what the world he lives in defines as capacity. Steinmetz in his laboratory proves unequal to Deerslayer in his wilderness. No matter how much lip service is paid to intellect and spirit, the primacy of the physical remains unbroken. The cripple can be granted endurance and fortitude. He can be sentimentalized into "worthiness," in much the same way as Dickens's Tiny Tim is worthy. But he is not a fit image for a young, vigorous nation.

The cripple who appears in American writing prior to the Civil War bridges a symbolic hiatus between what he is and what he reflects. And it is a distinctly American symbolism. Compare Melville's Captain Ahab to Dickens's Tiny Tim. Ahab is not merely physically crippled, his leg ripped from his body; he is crippled in the deepest spiritual sense. His injury subsumes his selfhood. His argument is not with what the white whale has done to him but with the fact of victimization. He rages not only against what he has lost but against his consciousness of that loss. He becomes an elemental force that threatens to overwhelm readers as he seems to have overwhelmed his creator, Melville. For he commands not only the action of the novel but a defiance so intense and single-minded that he remains to this day one of the great nay-sayers in all of literature.

But my purpose is not to discuss Ahab as archetypal rebel or satanic individualist. For me, Ahab is the essential cripple, a man whose sense of himself is dominated by physical insufficiency—like Richard, a "deformed, unfinished" man. For this Ahab, the question of whether the white whale represents principle or accident is less important than the rankling knowledge that what has happened has happened *to him*. It is *his* leg that has been ripped away by Moby Dick; it is *he* who must hobble through the world on an ivory substitute; and it is *he* who is doomed to live in a world in which accident has been thrust on him by something outside the self. And that something is a constant, unrelenting affliction to his consciousness of himself as a separate self.

Ahab remains the most powerful portrait of a cripple in all of American writing. In portraying a crippled "hero," Shakespeare is Melville's only rival. Melville never allows us to forget Ahab's missing leg. Ahab is not Job; he is not Lear; he is not even his biblical namesake. He is a New England whaling captain—*and he is a cripple*. He may resemble Job in that he assumes a mythic dimension even as we look to frame him more narrowly. Having abandoned normal life to seek vengeance on the white whale and having cut himself off from the ordinary ties that bind men to one another, he imposes his view of the world both on his crew and on the reader. His condition is so singular it can scarcely be understood by normal men and women, and yet he embodies his reader's afflictions, even the afflictions of the normal. He asks not for sympathy but for justice—and justice in his eyes is an act of vengeance, an insistence that only through an equality of fates can a cripple find true equality of condition.

Ahab's anguish is what he asks the reader to identify with. His defiance is purposeful and single-minded. Like Richard, he calls nature itself to account. And like Richard, too, he sees himself as frustrated power and potency, noble and maniacal in his insistence that he will bend nature itself if he has to. "Ahab stands alone among all the millions of the peopled earth, nor gods nor men his neighbors." In a world dominated by health and Emersonian self-reliance, Ahab is the maimed man who can trust only his own rage. He is the Demonic Cripple, calling others to account, insisting on righting fate by destroying the cause of the accident that crippled him. Like Richard, he sees himself as a man surrounded by schoolboys, a warrior in a world of weaklings:

> Why I, in this weak piping time of peace,
> Have no delight to pass away the time,
> Unless to see my shadow in the sun
> And descant on mine own deformity.

The Demonic Cripple inspires fear in his audience because others cannot really understand what drives his pursuit of vengeance. The normal sees accident or disease only in terms of its symbolism. The cripple sees what it has done to him. Where ordinary men and women who are crippled are expected to exist on the sufferance of the normals, tolerated with the visible infirmities they present, the Demonic Cripple is consumed by an isolation that goes beyond accident to harden into the very center of his existence. His spiritual opposite is the Charity Cripple, whose function is to perpetuate in his audience the illusion of its own goodness. One encounters the Charity Cripple in literature as one encounters him in a Jerry Lewis muscular dystrophy telethon, without risking anything of one's own substance.

And here, too, Melville provides the model. With Ahab in *Moby Dick* and Black Guineau in *The Confidence Man* Melville created the antipodal images that frame America's view of the cripple. Black Guineau is not, of course, the commanding figure Ahab is. Like the novel in which he appears, there is something scattered and drifting about him. As a character he is never fully realized. But as a type he is useful and interesting. The Demonic Cripple terrifies, the Charity Cripple soothes and entertains. As an object of compassion, a tool of the normal's smug superiority, he does not threaten the reader. Even the man who suspects that his sympathies are being manipulated and that he is the victim of a con enjoys the illusion of giving. He is quite frequently a willing victim.

More than any writer after Shakespeare, Melville had an imagination made vital by the split between appearance and reality. We are never altogether certain what is actually happening on board the steamboat *Fidele* in *The Confidence Man*. But we can easily recognize that in this masquerade the "grotesque Negro cripple" with a tambourine, begging from deck to deck, parodies the idea of the cripple as the recipient of other men's giving. Where Ahab commands, Black Guineau begs; where Ahab cries out for vengeance, Black Guineau whimpers after affection; where Ahab's wound adds to his physical presence, Black Guineau has been "cut down to the stature of a Newfoundland dog." His existence is offered to his fellow passengers as a "singular temptation to *diversion* and charity." He manipulates his fellow passengers because he recognizes that they are eager to lie to themselves, both about his condition as a cripple and about their own roles as players in the "game of charity."

Characters such as Black Guineau and Dickens's Tiny Tim entice the middle-class sentimentality of the nineteenth century. They charm because they relieve guilt. Of course, Melville was attacking that middle-class sentimentality, whereas Dickens shared it with his readers. The black cripple in *The Confidence Man* is a master of manipulation and disguise. The sole threat he possesses is his color, not his condition. He masquerades as a black man. Like the slave Babo in *Benito Cereno*, he transforms himself before our eyes, an object the other passengers can look at with compassion and charity. He is authentic in the same sense that Jerry's kids are authentic. Their faces may change, but the sole reason for their incapacity being demonstrated is to embarrass others into giving. As he catches pennies in his mouth, Black Guineau is the quintessential Charity Cripple. He demands our affection, not our respect. He insists on pity and compassion, assuming that dignity is itself a con. He offers relief to the giver, a totem of charity. His goodness is absorbed into public spectacle.

What the reader seeks from Black Guineau is the authentification of his own charitable impulses. Ahab's need to control others absorbs him. It is part of his quest. He must make the white whale as scarring to his crew as it was to him. The members of the crew of the *Pequod*, like the ship itself, are extensions of Ahab's will. Black Guineau has no will. He lives by begging, by filling us with the sense that it is our charitable impulses that protect the life of the cripple. He allows his audience to believe it will escape his fate.

The Charity Cripple soothes middle-class society because he refuses to take his wound as the source of his rage. Indeed, he refuses to acknowledge rage. His purpose is not to make the normal uncomfortable or guilty. He inspires pity, not fear. He plays with the heartstrings of the world. Or, rather, he plays on them. In making his audience feel good, he will destroy his own isolation as a cripple. He allows his audience to avoid the coldness of its own potential fate by becoming givers of alms. For the poor and the halt and the lame serve middle-class Christian sentimentality. Not only are they always with us, they can be called upon to help the middle class justify the power of its own virtue.

The antipodes Melville created in our national literature ultimately expanded, but they never really changed. To survey literary examples of physical disability would be boring and useless. I can think of few things that would mock literary history more savagely than a category of misfits and cripples. But it may be useful to look at some images of the cripple in American writing since Melville.

For the writers of the American Renaissance, who were born in pre–Civil War America, correspondences between physical and spiritual states were simply to be expected. The body reflected what the soul struggled with. But given the emergence of literary realism as the dominant literary mode after the Civil War, one might have expected a less symbolic cripple. To some extent, this is what happened. Both Ahab and Black Guineau were absorbed into what Howells defined as fiction's need to "cease to lie about life." But even a fiction that ceased to lie consciously managed to give voice to the myths men live by. Realism might have been intended as a way of looking at the world, but it inevitably became a way of thinking about what one found there.

Literary realism was never a mere approach to the craft of writing. Instead, it absorbed the writer's craft into a concern with how we live and what we live for. Realist writers might not wholly subscribe to the positivism that thrust modern scientific inquiry to the forefront of American intellectual life, but they did break with the symbolic and analogical modes of thinking that had shaped the American literary imagination prior to the Civil War. They were conscious of themselves as breaking new paths.

Unfortunately, the willingness to look is not synonymous with the ability to see. The cripple had never been invisible in America. But the moralistic symbolism the cripple's existence called forth not only distorted what the individual man or woman might be, it also distorted the background against which he or she was thrust. Both the Demonic Cripple and the Charity Cripple defined the cripple from outside their existence. The one image reflected the culture's fears and taboos, the other its sentimentality and aspirations. But neither reflected the life of the cripple as it was lived in America.

A nation that had been torn apart during an incredibly bloody Civil War had little choice but to look at the wounds of its sons who had fought that war. While the wounded hero had always been an attractive figure for writers, the realistic leavings of the war now came to our novelists and poets not as revelation but as legacy. The world had changed. And the cripple was absorbed into this more complex world, thrust against a less bucolic, darker landscape. The factories of the east and midwest, the large-scale agrarian industries that mocked the traditional family farm and awed Frank Norris at the turn of the century, the burgeoning financial capitalism that energized New York and Chicago and Philadelphia—what did these have in common with the forests and plains in which Natty Bumppo sought his fate?

Realist writers might have been expected to force Americans to look at the actual lives of those who were crippled. But the only palpable effect to be discovered in their work is a halfhearted attempt to bring the Demonic Cripple and the Charity Cripple together. In a novel such as Stephen Crane's *The Monster*, realism and sentimentality walk hand in hand. In Crane's novel, a Negro handyman saves a young boy from a fire, only to have his own face burned away and his mind destroyed in the rescue. Subsequently the Negro is defined as victim, a cripple, by a society he has served, a society to which he has little enough reason to be grateful. The novel fails, for the Negro's suffering is meant to ennoble but actually parodies. The Negro suffers as object lesson alone.

But what is perhaps most surprising about post–Civil War literature is how little of it actually depicts the visibly scarred and crippled. Rarely before or since has the American land been populated with so many victims of catastrophe. But the crippled are by and large ignored. It is as if the Civil War never happened. And when the maimed and wounded do appear, their disabilities prove not only unable to shape character but curiously peripheral to the possession of character. If we take as an example what has always seemed to me Howells's finest novel, *A Hazard of New For-*

tunes, we can see how tentative literary realism was in dealing with those who had been crippled during the war. Berthold Lindau is a German-born radical who has lost his left hand fighting against slavery in the Civil War. Lindau is among Howells's most complete characters, a man of great integrity and a certain harsh working-class nobility. In him Howells managed to create one of the few American fictional figures in whom political purpose and socialist ideology combine to produce a prophet of revolution.

Howells does not altogether approve of Lindau's political passions. One would think that he might humanize his character, make him less of an ideologue or at least illustrate the basis for his ideology, by focusing on Lindau's terrible wound. But the wound is an afterthought. The hand that has been shot away has little to do with Lindau. Too perceptive to believe that suffering makes individuals nobler, Howells still should have recognized that the kind of wound Lindau suffered was traumatic enough to shape his behavior in one way or another—to make him bitter, more determined to bring the revolution to fruition, more intent, even, on social justice. A more popular writer, Rebecca Harding Davis, could portray hunchbacked mill workers and consumptive poets as possessing an inner "goodness" because an unfeeling capitalism had made them cripples. Howells does the opposite. Whatever moral qualities Lindau claims derive from his politics, not his wound. Paradoxically, by more or less ignoring the missing hand Howells makes him one of the first truly realistic cripples in American literature. He anticipates such real-life crippled socialists as Helen Keller and Steinmetz. Lindau looks at his amputation as he looks at the Civil War itself, as no more than a symptom of an inherently unjust capitalism. The true kingdom—the one in which all disease will be conquered, all men made whole—will offer physical health to all. The dispossessed in Lindau's eyes are alone the economically dispossessed.

In looking at how the image of the cripple was projected in American literature, the period following the Civil War and lasting until the turn of the twentieth century puzzles. The images do not really leave a mark. They avoid Ahab's self-dramatization, just as they avoid Black Guineau's talent for making his own misery the world's debt. On the whole, however, they have more in common with the Charity Cripple than with the Demonic Cripple. (Lindau's rage has, as I have mentioned, little to do with his having been maimed in the war: What feeds his anger is his sense of the collective injustice done to working people the whole world over.) Like Crane's monstrous Negro, these images do not touch us. They are somehow too abstract, too thesis-ridden, and their pain is empty for the reader.

Even in Henry James one spies a curious reluctance to treat the crippled and the ill realistically. Perhaps this derives from his own back trauma. But characters who are ill and who appear in James's novels never seem altogether aware of their crippled or partial state. Ralph Touchett in *Portrait of a Lady* is an interesting character, but his disability has little to do with who he is. It simply provides James with a mechanical solution to the problem of how to make Isabel Archer an heiress. Millie Theale, the dying young heroine of *The Wings of the Dove*, stands among James's finest creations. But her illness and her death are both extraordinarily clean. She does not, at the end, "smell of drugs" or "taste of medicine," as Densher reminds Kate Croy. It is a beautiful death, deliberately set offstage in the novel. And it is impossible to think of Millie as ill. She looks too good, for one thing. And James wants us to believe that the question of whether Millie is ill enough to die is a question Millie alone can answer. No true cripple could possibly maneuver her fate with such freedom of choice.

More curious than the inability to portray disease and its effects realistically is that the cult of health was seized upon so avidly by American writers. Jack London, Frank Norris, even the tubercular Stephen Crane: in each we discover a post-Darwinian worship of physical power and strength. Although each was to die fairly young, it is significant that none of them saw the body as a mere physical manifestation of the Emersonian oversoul. Theirs is an adolescent dream of physical sexual perfectability. In *Vandover and the Brute* and *Moran of the Lady Letty*, Norris spoke for an entire literary generation obsessed with its discovery of the body. For such a group of writers, the cripple was bound to be an uncomfortable reminder of what the physical world actually was. His image was so drastically different from the image of the "blond beast" or the woman the blond beast loved and conquered that it could not be dealt with, either as reality or as image (with the exception of Crane's two-dimensional Negro monster).

Despite their realism, the writers who came of age in the 1890s belonged to one of the most romantic literary generations this nation has ever known. And like romantics throughout the ages, they worshiped strength and beauty—sometimes, strength *as* beauty. That they did this in the name of Zola and naturalism does not make them any less romantic. Biology was their religion. And if one worshiped strength and beauty, what possible interest could the cripple inspire? It was one thing to explore the lower depths of New York's Five Points and San Francisco's waterfront, for such places offered a young writer the opportunity to make his reputation as a man of experience. But what experience could he claim from the world occupied by cripples?

For the cripple was simply a victim. Or at least that was the image he projected. And it was an image that would not significantly change until after the Second World War. In the 1920s one still discovers the weak Charity Cripple, although the variations allowed his existence to grow more and more complex. He is still the victim, however, his character and fate determined by a world in which he is at best a spectator. The lives and ambitions of others bounce off his agony. In Ring Lardner's story "Champion," Midge Kelly scores his first knockdown on his crippled brother, Connie. Midge is a totally repellent character, and Lardner knows that his audience will recognize that to beat up a cripple is to demonstrate that one is the worst kind of bully. In Hemingway's *The Sun Also Rises*, Jake Barnes suffers a war wound that makes him sexually impotent and dooms him to the role of onlooker at the game of life. Jake watches as others act. Fitzgerald wrote about the young and the rich, a world that demands that even frailties be glamorous and marketable. Fitzgerald's characters may drink themselves into oblivion; they may crack up, die in airplane crashes, commit incest with their daughters—but they are not physically maimed. Like Millie Theale, they look good in their dying. Dos Passos sees physical disability as an extension of unjust social conditions, much as Howells's glum socialist Lindau does. And Dos Passos, a more gifted social observer than we are willing to recognize today, had difficulty in allowing his victims individuality. Even Faulkner, the most gifted of our writers and a novelist who wrote about the feebleminded and physically handicapped with the same intensity he brought to the creation of other residents of his fictional Yoknapatawpha County, rarely allowed them to step beyond the black humor of southern gothicism. They do not possess the courage of example, as, for instance, Dilsey does in *The Sound and the Fury*. Their symbolic representative is the impotent and deranged Popeye, whose refuge from physical and intellectual weakness takes the form of a gun and an absolutely blank moral sense.

Not until the 1930s and 1940s do we see a change in the attitude of American writers toward the crippled. In the work of such writers as Nathanael West, Dalton Trumbo, Nelson Algren, and Carson McCullers, cripples are undoubtedly horrific—but they are also singular, even commanding. They come increasingly to reflect the values of being an outsider for writers who have growing doubts about the society spawned by insiders. Perhaps the most excruciating portrait of a cripple in all of American literature is to be found in Trumbo's antiwar novel *Johnny Got His Gun*, published as the Second World War broke out in 1939. In a sense, one cannot discuss this novel as a book about a cripple, since the conditions of disability have been made so total that the novel exists beyond the territory occupied by any other fiction about the wounded. Joe Bonham, the novel's protagonist, is literally a basket case, who leaves everything but memory in the bloody trenches of France during the First World War. But a freak in a society interested in the freak as outsider is still a freak. His image remains linked to the Charity Cripple, for his task is to soothe even as he terrifies. And his life, like Black Guineau's, is designed so that it can be used by the larger society.

Yet since the end of the Second World War the cripple's image in literature has grown more complex and less demonic. Where Ahab threatened and Black Guineau parodied, the cripple now begins to root himself in the very world that once wished to be shielded from his presence. No longer as isolated or singular as he once was, he becomes one more embodiment of the facelessness of modern society, one more outcast in a world that has begun to find itself spiritually more comfortable with outcasts than with normals. He is what the critic Ihab Hassan has defined as the "rebel-victim," the protagonist of postwar American fiction who "mediates the contradictions of American culture by offering himself, in passive or demonic fashion, as scapegoat. His function is to create those values whose absence from our society is the cause of his predicament and ours."

This is not to claim that the cripple suddenly finds himself heroically defying an oppressive life-denying social system. It is simply to point out that victimization has been a powerful image in Western literature since the end of World War Two. Indeed, it might be said of us that we are a culture of victims. And in a culture in which group battles group for a kind of hegemony of suffering, the ability to endure becomes highly attractive. Endurance is itself defiance. The perversity of modern literature is that it pits the sufferings and misfortunes of one group against another. In this kind of race for credentials, the cripple discovers that his useless legs not only walk, they run. Is there anyone better equipped to speak of his life in terms of what Ernest Becker called "defiant self-creation"? Is there anyone better able to exploit the legacy that demonstrates to others that "an attack on all of life for what it has dared do to one" is nothing less than "a revolt against existence itself"?

The cripple's defiance springs from his recognition of what is absent in his life. Endurance is the price demanded of him over and over again. And yet, if endurance is all there is to life, then both the image he projects and the reality he feels will prove insufficient. His life is both comic and tragic, as emblematic as anyone's of what we have come to call, admittedly rather pontifically, "the human condition." The cripple can deal with his life not simply through rage at what has been taken but with recognition of what has been given. He is a debtor, but he discovers that his true debt is to himself. No more spiritual than the normal, he discovers that he needs to affirm and to deny as the normal does—although he also suspects that he has earned his right both to affirmation and denial as the normal has yet to do.

The writer who has probed the contradictions and paradoxes of contemporary American life most completely is Saul Bellow. No other writer has more insistently addressed his talents to probing who we are and how we got to where we are. It is not by accident, I suspect, that the realism Bellow employs to examine our America should produce the most complete portrait of a cripple in postwar American writing, William Einhorn, the poolroom owner and neighborhood politician of Augie March's Chicago.

Einhorn is by no means the central character in *The Adventures of Augie March*. He may not even be the most important secondary character in that exuberant novel. But in an essay discussing the cripple in American literature, how refreshing he is, the long-sought mediator between Black Guineau and Ahab, a man who looks over the table and takes whatever he finds there that is worth taking. Einhorn binds the audience not merely to his life but to the lives of all cripples. He can do this because he is stronger than those on whom he is dependent. And he is aware, as anyone who is crippled must be aware, that self-creation is limited by the very accidents that give it shape. Even irony may be another form of cowardice, a retreat from the obligations imposed by circumstance, unless it is tempered by the cripple's insistence that he has the right to try to manipulate what has until then manipulated him. Einhorn schemes, plots, lies, uses people. But he rarely lies to himself about the true prospects before him. For Bellow, Einhorn is an attractive character of dubious repute; for the cripple, he is a knowledgeable model, living with the contradictions inherent in his condition. Einhorn speaks to his own condition, *the cripple's condition*, as well as he speaks to his image:

> He wouldn't stay a cripple, Einhorn; he couldn't hold his soul in it. Sometimes, it was dreadful, this; he'd lose everything he'd thought through uncountable times to reconcile himself to it, and be like the wolf in the pit in the zoo who keeps putting his muzzle to the corners of the walls, back and forth, in his exhibition jail. It didn't happen often; probably not oftener than ordinary people get a shove of the demon. But it happened. Touch him when he was off his feed, or he had a cold or a little fever, or when there was a rift in the organization, or his posi-

> tion didn't feel so eminent and he wasn't getting the volume of homage and mail he needed—or when it was the turn of a feared truth to come up unseen through the multitude of elements out of which he composed his life, and then he'd say, "I used to think I'd either walk or swallow iodine, and I'd have massages and exercises, and drills when I'd concentrate on a single muscle and think I was building it up by my will, and it was all the bunk, Augie, the Coue theory, et cetera. For the birds. And *It Can Be Done* and the sort of stuff that bigshot Teddy Roosevelt wrote in his books. Nobody'll ever know all the things I tried before I finally decided it was no go. I couldn't take it, and I took it. And I *can't* take it, yet I do take it."

The image of the cripple in American writing has stopped here—with William Einhorn of Chicago, courtesy of Saul Bellow, now also of Chicago. In the three and a half decades since the appearance of Bellow's *The Adventures of Augie March* there have been any number of portraits of cripples in our literature. There have been writers for whom the sense of physical handicap has been more central than it could possibly be for Bellow. There have certainly been writers who have dealt with the theme more dramatically, cutting closer to the bone than Bellow could. But Bellow is the image-maker. No other writer has been better able to record the follies and aspirations of men and women in this America as they enumerate the many ways of being an American in the modern world. The country Bellow depicts in his novels and stories has an excessive view of itself. Einhorn's scarred uniqueness is certainly more satisfactory than the puffery and pretension of modern American life. God knows, he has his shortcomings. But in speaking of Einhorn's crippled condition Bellow addresses the inevitable struggle of all those men and women whose sense of their own incompleteness threatens an adulthood otherwise well earned. Einhorn has his failures as a man and as an image.

But he is man rather than metaphor, trapped within his contradictions as much as he is trapped within a body that cannot fulfill what his imagination demands.

Einhorn stands between the Charity Cripple and the Demonic Cripple. His physical helplessness neither ennobles nor damns him. And he remains an example of what other writers can do with the figure of the cripple. His vision is actually quite narrow, as he bores in on the singular self trying to get through his life with the sense that he, rather than disease, has defined it. Or, rather, that he has defined it in conjunction with disease. In his voice, a surprisingly ordinary voice, the reader hears "yes" and "no" and "maybe." His state, the state of the cripple who cannot do what the normal can do, is a beachhead from which he attacks the world. He anchors his existence to the task of controlling his fate by controlling his needs—and this from a man who is "helpless."

Einhorn has come through, he is a survivor. And survival, as Faulkner noted in his fictions, is the state most deserving of our admiration. Einhorn thrusts his presence into a world filled with men and women who are no more fulfilled than he is but who will never know the reason why. Einhorn knows that each man, sick or well, seeks to revenge himself on fate, to take back what has been taken away by a blind, quixotic universe. He is not so far removed from Ahab and Richard as we might like to believe. There is always, as he tells Augie, that inevitable moment "when you feel like the stinking fly in the first cold snap." At most other moments, survival is distinction enough, and awareness of the price he has paid for that survival is what separates Einhorn from "normal" people.

Survival against formidable odds becomes an end in itself, an image appealing to an age in which little else can assume the proportions of the heroic. The Survivor Cripple gets by on his endurance, his wit, his insistence on manipulating a world which insists on its right to define him, and his courage. He gets by without the expectation of any reward greater than getting by. As isolated as Ahab and as manipulative as Black Guineau, he understands the comedy of his situation. The only model available to him is what he finds in his own life. The landscape, wilderness and all, has long since passed Natty Bumppo by. It exists now only in the imagination. And who is better able to seize it than the man who has had to imagine his life into existence?

Hineni

In September of 1941, when I was eight, my father moved our family from the large three-bedroom apartment in the Bronx that we shared with my grandmother, two uncles, and three cousins to a small one-bedroom apartment of our own a block away. On the same day that he signed the first and last lease he would take out in this America, he walked down to Hull Avenue and enrolled me in the beginner's class of the Mosholu Jewish Center Hebrew School.

Neither decision threatened to change my life significantly—at least not on the surface. The small apartment was little more than the length of a football field from our old apartment, and the boys with whom I went to cheder at three-thirty every afternoon were my friends and classmates at P.S. 80.

But, however gently, I had been uprooted. The distance between 3150 Rochambeau Avenue and 315 East 206th Street was fraught with the tension of the new and the threat of the unexpected. The lessons of city streets invariably derive from a geography of the familiar and unfamiliar. We were leaving a street that was Jewish and Eastern European and toned by the Yiddish immigrant experience, for a street that was Catholic and Irish and self-consciously American. There would be new lessons to be learned and new prices to be paid. For a city boy in 1941, to ignore that was to deny the way of the world.

The lessons began that very first afternoon I came home from cheder, a red siddur and a blue writing tablet with a bearded and turbaned face on its cover in my hand. Mr. Danzig, my Hebrew school teacher, identified the face as that of Maimonides, the great Rambam himself, but the Irish boys my age waiting for me on 206th Street were convinced it was the face of the Jewish God. After that first fight to keep possession of my prayer books, I decided that face might as well be "our" God as anyone else. It had brought me my first ethnic fight; it was the first time I heard myself labeled "Christ killer"; it had enlisted me in the struggle between "us" and "them," a permanent foot soldier in the armies of Jehovah.

The experience was certainly not traumatic. I was big for my age, and I didn't dislike fighting. In fact, I was a lot more worried about what my older cousin Leo might do to me if he ever heard I had run from a fight than I was of the four or five boys trying to grab my siddur, convinced I had killed their Christ. Having begun Hebrew school only an hour earlier, I was filled with fervor for "my side." And so I easily slipped into the role of defender of the faith.

Besides, I had been brought up to expect exactly such distinctions between "us" and "them." On Rochambeau Avenue we were constantly warned to be wary of those who were not Jews. For "us," the goyim were not so much people as category—a thick wall that mysteriously appeared out of nowhere to block our way. The wall had to be avoided, for it might very easily collapse and take us down with it. Simply put, non-Jews were not to be trusted—except, of course, for the Irish teachers at P.S. 80, who, being teachers, deserved all the respect and reverence we could muster.

That afternoon I also became aware of the presence of faith. When he called attendance, Mr. Danzig told us to answer not "present"—which was how we answered roll call at P.S. 80—but "*hineni*," a word he carefully enunciated by pressing his tongue against his large white teeth. "Heee-nehhh-neee," he said. And we boys faithfully emulated him, thrusting tongue against teeth to invoke a language stamped with God's own tongue of fire.

"What does it mean?" someone asked hesitantly.

"It means 'here I am,' " answered Mr. Danzig proudly. "It is how we Jews answer God's call. Like our father, Abraham."

I knew nothing then about my father Abraham. And in the weeks that followed, as I returned from Hebrew school to the ritual confrontations awaiting me almost daily, I even began to have my doubts about the bargain Mr. Danzig was intent on striking between God and me. Still, I was a pliable eight-year-old, a natural-born drifter whose opinions had no true edge and whose ambitions were circumscribed by talents to which he could assign a fixed American value. But even though I was quite willing to accept whatever was meted out to me, the Jews I revered were named Hank Greenberg and Barney Ross and Sid Luckman, not Abraham and Isaac and Jacob.

In the weeks that followed, I came to like those Irish boys, who, after the ritual battle for possession of the Jewish God had been concluded, would urge me to get my roller skates and join them for a twilight game of street hockey in the cold autumn air. And I came to enjoy my lessons in cheder. I liked the sound of that strange language, the language God had spoken to Moshe Rabbenu, and I discovered a surprising affinity for davening.

I would sneak out of the Saturday morning children's services, to which my father insisted I go, usually to get to a baseball or football game on time. But sometimes I would sneak upstairs to the main sanctuary, where I would sequester myself behind the oak doors and listen to the chanting of the old men. The chanting filled me with comfort tinged by sadness. Of course, I had no idea what they were praying for. But I loved the sound of their davening. In September, 1942, after I had been in cheder for a year and long after my fights with those Irish boys had petered out into the truce of guarded friendships, I accompanied my father to the main sanctuary for Rosh Hashanah and Yom Kippur services. There I took unexpected pleasure in watching the old men bend low into their oversized *talaysim*, ancestral gestures in which they buried their bodies in preburial shrouds, sanctifying not God's name or mystery but the act of homage itself.

I don't mean that I was searching for God's presence. I didn't feel it, and I wasn't looking for it. What I felt was what I wanted to feel—Jews enmeshed in their own collective myth. The palpable touch of some prehistoric past enfolded me, momentarily warding off rumors that already, in 1942, were beginning to emerge from war-ravaged Europe about the fate of our people.

I was, I now see, asking ritual to absorb me into the collective presence, the very tone of existence Mr. Danzig had evoked when he fervently recited the story of Abraham's sacrifice of Isaac. Years later I listened to Elie Wiesel speaking at the 92nd Street Y into a repository of silence so thick I felt as if I could literally touch it. Wiesel told how his father had recited the story of Abraham's sacrifice of Isaac on a train taking the two of them to Auschwitz.

For me, as if stamped on every moment of our history as a people, the word "*hineni*" burned with the promise of redemption, more powerful than the nightmare of Auschwitz, more necessary than the lamb sent by God to replace Isaac. *Hineni*. Here I am. The word had become for me a passport to that God I already suspected I could never believe in. "*Hineni*" embodied selfhood and responsibility; "*hineni*" carried one into the community; "*hineni*" transformed the child into the man.

Unable to believe, I knew, even at the age of nine, that I was doomed to be a Jew. Unwilling to live up to the demands of what I could not believe in, I cultivated ritual and even prayer. Unaware of the need for illusion in any individual life, I sought proof not of God's existence but of my belonging. "*Hineni*" embodied the contradictions I could not live with and, at the same time, captured the sense of community I did not want to live without.

In July, 1944, some six weeks after the invasion of France, I caught polio. I spent the next two years of my life as a patient in the appropriately named New York State Reconstruction Home in West Haverstraw, and, during that time, expanded my argument with the God in whom I did not believe. The believer who falls seriously ill finds God's presence in the pain to which he must bear witness; the nonbeliever, on the other hand, insists that God's absence is confirmation enough that suffering is a simple accident. But both believer and nonbeliever discover that illness makes the idea of God curiously personal.

About a month before I was scheduled to return to 206th Street, I found myself moving in my wheelchair past a room we boys knew as the Isolation Room. The occasional patient sent there was deliberately shielded from our eyes. Cloaked in the power of their suffering, they would simply appear, never to communicate with us, hidden behind closed doors through which frosted panes of glass allowed a febrile smoky light that succeeded in making the mysterious more mysterious.

In the hierarchy disease establishes, patients in the Isolation Room were beyond our sense of ourselves. We never knew precisely what they "had." Sequestered away, they filled us with fear. We other boys would wheel in packs past the closed door with the frosted glass panes, and we would automatically avert our eyes and lower our voices, pushing as hard as possible to get quickly beyond what threatened us.

Two weeks earlier, a new boy had arrived in the Isolation Room. No one remained for more than a month or six weeks before being sent on. It was a place of passing through—toward death, we assumed, although we rarely mentioned that possibility, even to each other. Out of the corners of our eyes we would watch doctors and nurses move in and out of that room in a silence that carried a weight of its own. And in that self-consciously tough manner adolescents adopt when dealing with death, we would gather in wheelchairs on the bricked-in porch of the ward, like movie cowboys on tethered horses, and speculate on what was wrong with our latest guest.

On this particular afternoon, the door to the Isolation Room had been accidentally left open. Instead of fastening my eyes on the floor and pushing past as quickly as I could, I impulsively looked up. Two of the nurses were working on the mysterious patient. They had turned his paralyzed body on its side, and one of them held him positioned like that while the other gently washed him.

His back was naked and I could see the outline of every bone ripped with bedsores and blisters, and raw blotches of skin dappled, like a Pollock canvas, purple and red and yellow and fish-belly white. Even where prostheses and broken limbs were the norm, the sight was horrifying. Unable to take my eyes from that back, I stared until the nurse washing him angrily gestured me away with the wet washcloth in her hand. Through it all, the boy remained mute. I wheeled down the corridor to the lavatory, where I went into one of the toilet stalls and threw up.

And then I heard myself sobbing, crying out in rage to that God who could not exist because his presence would be an endorsement of the meaning of accident. As I write this now, I am increasingly uncomfortable. Fifty-three-year-old writers are supposed to be beyond the need to question God's presence. Having lived through the discovery of the Holocaust and the revelations about the gulags and the nuclear destruction of Hiroshima and Nagasaki, I tell myself that an upstate farm boy's skin covered by raw bedsores from three years of lying paralyzed in bed with a broken back is simply of little consequence. After all, this was just a year after the pictures of heaped-up arms and legs and bodies from the death camps had emerged from Europe. It was less than a year since Hiroshima had been leveled in a few seconds. And yet those canvases are still too huge.

What I wanted—what, I now know, I still want—was something to assume the personal burden of the world's pain. And, in some mysterious way I would never understand, I had latched onto that boy's silent, bitter, ungrieving movement toward death. It was as if his imminent death had assumed responsibility for my inability to believe. I wanted to hear him, too, cry out, "*Hineni!*"

The word had become my talisman. Whenever I tried to define my curious and contradictory relationship to Judaism and being a Jew, "*hineni*" came to mind. I had been transformed into the atheist who envisions himself going to his death with the *Shema* on his lips. Denying the possibility of God, I became a believing nonbeliever. I still am. Even as I deny, I join my fellow Jews in the synagogue each Yom Kippur in a collective plea that the God I do not believe in absolve us from our sins as a people. I deny the meaning of specifically religious traditions, and then, to the amazement of my friends, insist that my sons be bar mitzvahed.

Distrusting theology, I believe that God should struggle, as we do, to free himself from his own domination. Denying belief, I feel myself collapse into history—praying my way not into faith but into myth—seeking to match my expectations for the human.

And so I still find myself, as I did when I was eight years old and fighting on the street for the honor of that Jewish God, defending what I know I can never possess. Offended by the sense of certainty that seizes friends, Christian and Jew, who are believers, I find myself envious of those who have rediscovered faith and returned to the religious fold. I feel that I have missed out on something essential when, on Yom Kippur or Rosh Hashanah, my gaze scans the synagogue until it fixes on the face of a single worshiper for whom, I decide, belief has never been a problem or is a problem long since settled, a face rapt in a kind of worship I will never know. And my mind cries out, "No!" even as my spirit cries out, "*Hineni!*"

There can be no belief without faith—and it is precisely faith I lack. Perhaps it is no more than the envy of one who lacks what others have, but I discovered here a less than comforting note about the faith of many who, having found God, are intent on never giving him up again. Even as they invoke humility, they lack the tolerance of doubt. My doubt—and the doubt of others like me. Not tolerance of the doubter—they were all too willing to give me that—but of doubt itself.

Beneficiaries of "the truth," they are convinced it is available to all for the asking. Maybe it is. But I find that what a good deal of their belief comes down to, in the final analysis, is the attempt to divide men and women into believers and nonbelievers, saved and damned.

I suppose such an attitude comes naturally to those who repossess belief. Their impatience with those of us who cannot get beyond our doubt is certainly understandable. The impatience of Orthodox Jews with those who, like me, consider themselves "cultural Jews" is natural. We Jews have never been comfortable with theology. What we revere is the Law. The Orthodox Jew's sense of me as an imposter—the man who insists on his right to say "*hineni*" even as he denies the God who demands "*hineni*" of him—is formidably logical.

No matter what pleasure I may take in ritual, no matter how deep and soothing the memory of old men davening, I simply do not believe. Abraham accepted the consequences of saying "*hi-*

neni" by accepting God as the word's source. I do not because I cannot.

When, as a graduate student in the 1950s, I tried to take that leap of faith Kierkegaard and Buber made so appealing, I found nothing but the continuation of my gnawing doubt. And the doubt remained wedded to that skin-peeled broken back of the silent boy in the Isolation Room who was waiting to die. He still had time to serve before death claimed him. And, in my mind's eye, I still pray to that God I don't believe in that he went down defiantly, unrepentant to the end.

"He wouldn't open his mouth," sighed Miss Cunningham, the lovely blond nurse who had angrily gestured me away from the door with the wet washcloth in her hand. It was a week later, the day after the boy with the broken back had been sent away from the New York State Reconstruction Home, and we were sitting in her office. Neither Nurse Cunningham nor I knew where he had been sent, and neither of us wanted to know. In another two weeks, I myself would be going home to the neighborhood in the Bronx where both Eastern European Jews and Irish Catholics had been praying for two years for my recovery. "I've never known a more obstinate boy," she said. "Never said a word. Not to anyone. You'd think a boy like that would pray. But it was just silence in that room."

I didn't say anything. And along with the other boys in the ward, I immediately stopped talking about the boy in the Isolation Room. I was preparing for my own return to 206th Street. But I didn't stop thinking about him, maybe because I sensed I would need his presence back home in the Bronx even more than I needed it here. His silence had been a way of resisting, of refusing to be swallowed up by the accidental evil of an indifferent universe. I admired him. I admired him as much as I have ever admired anyone.

He was tough, tougher than I would ever be. What Nurse Cunningham saw as obstinacy, I already saw as the courage of denial. Had he lived in Abraham's time, he, too, might have been inspired by faith and cried "*hineni*" to a demanding God.

Hineni. Here I am. In the years that followed, the word would come to mean for me not willingness to acknowledge God's command but that point in a man's life when he chooses to resist suffering—both his own and the suffering of others—because the refusal to cry out is the only affirmation he can make of the human in himself.

Hineni. Here I am. It could be voiced by nonbelievers, too, its magic a proclamation of defiance as well as acceptance. Perhaps its legacy was never meant exclusively for the religious. *Hineni.* Here I am. With my doubt, my lack of faith, my silence—and my defiance. Another Jew, answering the call.

From the burning bush

The autobiographical "I"

I have never known a writer who did not desire to redress the facts of his life through the practice of his art. It is a need that resonates in the myths that nurture the craft we practice. Adam naming the animals God parades before him in the book of Genesis offers a mythic paradigm for the writer discovering the power of his voice. Standing in his newness in the Garden of Eden, Adam is an innocent blessed with the command of language, and this green and fecund and breathing world of being in every shape and form passes in salute before him.

> And out of the ground the Lord God formed every beast of the field and every fowl of the air: And brought *them* unto Adam to see what he would call them. And whatsoever Adam called every living creature, that was the name thereof.
>
> And Adam gave names to all cattle, and to the fowl of the air, and to every beast of the field.

In this scene Adam is the archetypal writer—a namer of names. We see the world as he ordains we see it, as if without Adam's ability to name the earth and its creatures we could not be made human through language. And it is language that transforms man himself from animal to human being, just as it is language that endows the writer with his power to name.

As appealing as Adam's naming of the animals is, it remains, I must confess, too bucolic a view of the writer's function to suit my taste. I prefer a different Old Testament myth, one in which the voice turns out to be more grating, resonant with doubt and stress and worry about the writer's ability to name the world accurately. For even as he shapes his voice to the demands of the world, the writer struggles with the need to test his language before those whom he views—and who, in turn, view him—with suspicion and even hostility.

In expressing my preference for that splendid scene in which Moses stands before the burning bush, I may simply be confessing to the continued hold that my own origins exert on me. I grew up in the post-immigrant New York of the forties and fifties, a city in which opportunity and skepticism were equally bred in the bone. Long before the idea of becoming a writer entered my mind, I had already suspected that a life worth writing about had to contain a secret, some experience that one could claim as one's own. By the age of seven, I suspected that a life without such a secret simply wasn't worth knowing. The streets of the city taught me that; Mark Twain taught me that; later, unknown writers with pseudonymous names in pulp magazines called *Amazing Stories* or *Fantastic Adventures* taught me that; newspaper comics and radio serials taught me that; most of all, a Hollywood fed on the same immigrant aspirations I had been fed on taught me that.

Adam's naming of the animals as God parades them before him was simply too pacific an image for a child of the city who already suspected that without struggle there could be no self, not even an imaginary self. One had to fight to possess even dreams and fantasies—at least in New York one did. And that, I am convinced, remains the reason why Moses standing before the burning bush on Mount Horeb continues to embody for me both the individual's struggle to claim a self and the writer's struggle to claim a voice of his own. At this point in my life it has become increasingly difficult to differentiate the one from the other.

In the text, Moses flees from Egypt after he has killed an overseer who is beating a Hebrew slave. Moses acts in a blind rage, and by his action he transforms himself from prince of Egypt to runaway Hebrew slave—and a slave who has the added, if dubious, distinction of being a murderer. Moses escapes to Midian, where, as a reward for helping the daughters of Jethro water their father's flock, he is given the hand of Jethro's oldest daughter, Zipporah, in marriage.

At this point in the story we confront one of those biblical breaks in the narrative that remain redolent with the mystery of time passing. We learn little about Moses' years in Midian, other than that Zipporah bears him a son, Gershom, and that he keeps his father-in-law's flocks beneath the shadow of Mount Horeb. But narrative, particularly biblical narrative, signifies as much by what is left out as by what is included. Ever since I first read this story as a child, I have imagined different roles for Moses during this passage of time. Even today I like to allow my imagination to dwell on those mysterious years in the desert. Think of Moses growing older, a kind of desert pre-bourgeois. Envision a man who in our time might be a contented reader of Mann or Tolstoy—responsible, industrious, sober, a stern but loving father and husband, a disciplined keeper of his father-in-law's sheep. But not a man seeking decisive change. Note how hard he tries to counter the voice from the burning bush as it insists he return to

Egypt and free his fellow Hebrews through his command of God's word. Even the most casual textual explication shows that Moses wants no part of Egypt or of Pharaoh or of his fellow Hebrews.

Moses is here the archetypal writer because we see him struggling to possess his own voice. He argues with the voice of God. He is not a warrior seeking battle or a prophet equating God's demands with his own nagging sense of mission. No, he is simply one more soldier in the ranks who sees no reason to volunteer. He remains uncertain of his talent. He does not know whether he possesses the words to do what God expects him to do. And his insistence on bargaining with the voice—a bit cranky, more than a bit skeptical—indicates that he prefers the security of the everyday and settled to this fiery call to glory.

It is a splendid scene, filled with ambivalent urges. On the one hand Moses reluctantly accepts the need to discover his own voice, the writer's voice; on the other, he is overwhelmed by awe and worship, for he recognizes in the voice emanating from the burning bush the dreadful power of language. Moses seeks reality, not divinity. But he knows that a voice of his own will make him a rival to that very God who commands the voice he possesses.

By definition a writer's voice is ambiguous. And it is particularly ambiguous when the writer attempts to speak for a reality he himself has not directly experienced. The Moses who pleads that the Hebrew slaves will not listen to him because of his defects of speech and presence is a model for the writer—especially the American writer. Suspicious of the new as he is, without a common culture, other than a memory of their suffering, to bind him to his fellow Hebrews, who can blame him for wanting to remain with his wife, his son, and his father-in-law's flocks beneath Mount Horeb?

Moses does not want to confuse his business with God's. But

when asked how he should identify the source of his mission to the Hebrew slaves, Moses hears the voice from the burning bush cry out: "I am that I am!"

For a writer, not only is the scene immensely rich, but it is also personally threatening. Here is Moses, our archetypal scribe, barefoot, awestruck, standing alone on consecrated ground. In the midst of fear and dread, he must also feel himself burning with envy at the injustice that prevents him too from being able to pronounce those magic words "I am." Even after Moses returns to Egypt, having first conned God into sending along his brother Aaron as a kind of verbal aide-de-camp (which, I suppose, makes Aaron the first editor), we sense that he is still grumbling beneath his breath, irritated that it is God rather than the writer who is able to say "I am." For, like all subsequent writers, Moses must have recognized that only God can take possession of the pronoun "I"; only God can claim the exclusive self by the definitive words "I am." Adam was allowed to name the animals, but the real writer, like Moses, wants a voice singular enough that he can name the Self.

Writers in Bristol and Lagos and Alicante and Lima are undoubtedly as concerned with their ability to construct a singular voice as are writers in New York and Duluth and Austin and San Francisco. And yet one must brave the threat of provincialism and call attention to the sense of difference facing the American writer in this, too. For it is not merely the writer's ability to claim an authentic self through the use of his literary voice that is at issue here in America. It is also his ability to command a voice that allows opposites to clash while remaining faithful to the demands of verification, accuracy, and contradiction that is the true issue for the writer in America. The serious American writer discovers that he is expected to speak for the aspirations of the culture as well as for the aspirations of the self. He seeks a voice that will allow him to narrate events in their proper sequence but that will also allow him to anchor himself to the drama of the nation through those events. Like it or not, he is Emerson's "transparent eyeball"—and what he sees reflected in the nation's destiny is his own essential self.

But if our writers have been transparent eyeballs, what they best reflected was the first-person singular, even when they clothed that creature in fiction. In Europe the writer's voice seemed as much the property of the culture as of the individual. But our best American writers have seemed intent on projecting the absolute "I" from the voice they adopted, as if they were wrestling like Jacob with his angel for the godlike being within.

The tone was already apparent in the nineteenth century. Even as Europe grew increasingly impatient with the idea of the individual, America produced such conscious I-sayers as Emerson, Thoreau, and Whitman. Had he been a European poet, Whitman's autobiographical imperative would have sounded ludicrous. In fact it was the specifically American quality of his voice that led to his being taken up in Europe and England by every baked and half-baked seer or prophet who found in Whitman's example a passage through to his own contradictory longings. It also led other Europeans to see him personifying what Wyndham Lewis termed "that great American baby." Whitman's voice clearly and insistently serves the self. But Whitman considered that self to be serving the nation. What would seem bombastic in a European writer seems altogether natural in him, a way of claiming the autobiographical "I."

> I celebrate myself and sing myself,
> And what I assume you shall assume,
> For every atom belonging to me as good belongs to you.

In the opening lines of what has since come to be seen as the most aggressively American poem ever written, Whitman lets us know that his achievement of a distinctively personal voice is both his triumph and America's triumph. The "I" of autobiography allows the poet to set himself up as God's rival. Anyone who read "Song of Myself" at a young enough age can still remember how he reverberated not to the lines but to the sense that he had come into the presence of a godlike being. I was not quite eighteen when I first read the poem. And what thrilled me then—and, let me confess, still thrills me today—was the poet's incredible ability to declare a self. It may be, as I have heard more than one critic insist, that these lines are bad poetry. But the voice is a great voice, a writer's voice, an American voice. And it demands our attention in a poem as unmistakably American as Goethe's *Faust* is European.

The voice in "Song of Myself" is absolute, like the voice Moses hears from within the burning bush. It is also remarkably embracing, for the only rival the poet can acknowledge as enemy is the world that exists beyond his own sense of himself. Like God, Whitman claims for himself the authority of self-creation. Adam's naming of his fellow creatures is matched by Whitman's insistence that he is both lion and deer, hunter and prey. The words "I am" are certainly not foreign to his bearded, androgynous lips. In line after line of "Song of Myself" "I am" finds its echo. Even chosen at random, the lines shout with the poet's insistence on his own primacy.

> I am the mate and companion . . .
> I am of old and young . . .
> I am the poet of the Body and I am the poet of the Soul . . .
> I am the poet of the woman the same as the man . . .
> I am the hounded slave . . .

As poetry, the best that can be said of these lines is that their success is mixed. But "Song of Myself" stands as a great autobiographical poem because as a whole, as a life, it is so much more powerful, so much more moving, than the simple reduction to its lines. Whitman offers us a series of scenes in which we recognize not the making of an American but the making of all Americans. The poet creates himself as the country itself was created—vast, sweeping, never fully formed. And yet he is never immodest. His voice is unique not only because it is his but because he uses it to speak for all other Americans. He is not trying to be a democratic Christ when he writes, "I am the man, I suffer'd, I was there." He is simply trying to absorb the nation within the writer's voice.

Other American writers have been more modest. Even as they speak autobiographically, they are obsessed not merely with the self but with the places the self inhabits. The writer measures himself and his America. Reality is thwarted by possibility. And roads one has been unable to take loom larger and larger in the imagination. One discovers that one might not sell his soul for wealth or power, but one also discovers that alternatives pursue one in dreams even as they recede in actual possibility. My own vision of thwarted selves, for example, of what I might have become had I not been crippled by polio at the age of eleven, makes me suspect that I very well might sell my soul—assuming, of course, that I could find the proper taker—for the chance to do something as banal as hit a baseball once again or feel myself running through a landscape that probably never existed except in my childhood's eye.

For the obsession with the self in its places matched against the alternative self in its unfulfilled moments remains both the fulfillment of autobiographical writing and the greatest danger facing the autobiographical writer. Excessive self-consciousness can destroy the re-creation of a life. And trying to relive the past that is never quite the past one wanted carries its own obvious consequences. The conflict between who one is and whom one might have wanted to be can also be the source of the writer's deepest, most useful tensions.

I have never been able to believe that an autobiographer's life should be an open book—or that the purpose of writing about that life is to provide society with a model of what to do or what not to do. And yet that is the ostensible purpose of what remains the best-known of all written American lives, *The Autobiography of Benjamin Franklin*. Franklin exploits a voice that is solid, simple, and ordinary, an autobiographical voice that makes us think its author possesses precisely those virtues.

Every obstacle in life could be conquered, every defeat transformed into what contemporary psychological popularizers like to call "a personal growth opportunity." For Franklin, the American self was the true American faith. No one ever worked harder to show his compatriots how to make themselves better. The man would have been at home not only in the America of Dale Carnegie but in the America of Lee Iacocca and Jack La Lanne, too. For he understood, as if by instinct, that the proper voice for his fellow Americans was a voice resonant with simplicity, clarity, and accuracy. The writer's job was simply to create the record of the writer's life. And in Franklin's case that record consisted of the very substantial achievement of the man who used his simplicity and practicality and solid Americanness to become the darling of eighteenth-century Parisian aristocracy.

At its best, Franklin's rational optimism evolved into a powerful national religion that still commands our attention. At its worst, it created a parody of its own shallowness. His autobiography remains a book against which every subsequent American writer who chose to engage his readers in the first-person voice has had to measure his own achievement. To reread the *Autobiography* today is to understand what so infuriated Melville that he has the hero of *Israel Potter*, a common man, slam down one of the

"Poor Richard" pamphlets in disgust and cry out, "It's wisdom that's cheap and it's fortune that's dear." Melville recognized, as Lawrence recognizes in his *Studies in Classic American Literature*, that if one chose to write about one's American self in a distinctively American voice, then the savage contradictions abounding in American life should at least be sounded in the accents. In Franklin's autobiography they aren't.

The standard criticism of Franklin as a writer, that he lacked a conception of evil and knew absolutely nothing about the darker side of human nature, can be admitted without destroying the essential validity of the man's life or of the book he created from that life. For such limitations the man can easily be forgiven—particularly by a time which may pay too much attention to the dark side of human nature. Ours is still a philosophically pragmatic country where a man is what a man does. And one reason Franklin adopted a voice that had no room for evil is that he was determined to teach his fellow Americans how to succeed. In reading the *Autobiography* one has the impression that Franklin wanted to set his life before his compatriots as if it could be reduced to a mathematical proposition. Since what a man did was what a man was, the autobiographer's task was simply to describe what he had done in the process of making his life his. Let others worry about the nature of evil; let continental philosophers concern themselves with questions of metaphysics. Franklin was content to teach his audience how to put out fires in the streets of Philadelphia and how to create a lending library that might serve all citizens.

Perhaps Franklin was one of those rare autobiographers to whom the imaginary other life and the alternative kind of achievement simply offer no temptation. Perhaps the only measure the man needed was the picture he saw before him, the lives lived by his fellow Americans. The truth is that Franklin may think of his voice as the voice of the ordinary man, but it is actually the voice of the ordinary man's teacher. There is something missing from Franklin's autobiography, something essential, an absence not merely of the deeper self but of the very possibility of a deeper self. Perhaps this is simply to say that the man who wants to present himself as an example to others in some essential manner ceases to be seen as a man at all. No one, I take it, would say of Franklin's autobiography, "Who touches this touches a man."

But if Franklin is unwilling to admit to the rage and anger all of us must feel simply in order to get through our days, his is still the first distinctively American voice in our literature. Franklin refused to transform felt experience into a personal argument with the universe. *The Education of Henry Adams*, by contrast, is the work of a writer who seems incapable of doing anything else. Adams was more than willing to grapple with the metaphysical underpinnings of this universe. It was, after all, a universe which had failed him at birth.

Adams's *Education* has always seemed to me a book that petulantly asks that one respond to its author in a deeply personal way. I find Adams one of the least attractive figures in American literary history, a man who managed to elevate the cultural whine into a principle of literary composition—at least in the *Education*. There is about the voice Adams chooses for the *Education* a note of consistent irritation, and there is a sense in which the book itself seems not so much an autobiography as a series of notes by a perpetually bright schoolboy for whom intelligence was no more than a way of bribing the gods. Adams's rejection of the personal, of intimacy of any sort, results in a crabbed tightness, as if the autobiographer had adopted a voice not out of any passion to commit himself to the page but out of a desire to indict his compatriots for the unforgivable sin of being able to admire the energy of a Grant while rejecting the sensibility of an Adams.

My focus here should not be on my own distaste for Adams; it should instead be on how the voice he assumes in the *Education* conveys the writer's autobiographical sense of himself. From that perspective the qualities that irritate me serve the writer well. A bit withdrawn, more than a bit skeptical, Adams balances his instinct for self-preservation with his need to explain his "failure" as an American of the modern world. He is a victim rather than a leader, and the chief villain of the *Education* turns out to be modernity itself. Adams sufficiently controls his voice so that he succeeds, with most readers at least, in persuading us that the distaste we may feel for him is actually a distaste for the country and the times that together have made him so finely tuned a victim. The writer's voice in this autobiography is sardonic and distant, playful and serious—but always a voice focusing on the need for self-justification.

I find it curious that *The Education of Henry Adams* continues to be viewed as a book re-creating one of the great American lives. Adams shies away from self-revelation not merely through some lingering ancestral distaste but because, had he written about the undisguised, naked self, he might have been forced to question more closely the supposed failure of the times in which he lived. Because Adams fails to reconcile his life's failure with the world's, he also fails to make of himself the embodiment of that failure—and not, as he claimed, because he was unable to emulate St. Augustine and move from multiplicity to unity but because he was least American in his sense of failure as triumph. There is something furtive and secretly vengeful about the voice Adams adopts in the *Education*—as if even in confession he cannot bring himself to forgive his fellow Americans for having made a would-be public man wait and wait for the call that never came.

Whatever else can be said of Lincoln Steffens's autobiography, its author remains a far more attractive figure than Henry Adams. Here is a man genuinely willing to take whatever he can from a world he may find puzzling but never uninteresting. Steffens is a sojourner eager to confront the chaos Adams found so threatening. He will take the world the way it comes. If it comes in the form of the fascism of that "divine dictator" Mussolini or the iron-fisted communism of Lenin or the rapacious capitalism of the robber barons, that is simply the world's way. Steffens sees his task simply: He must set down his bewilderment as he tries, as he wrote, to "unlearn all my learning." The trouble is that he is forever reaching for the nearest answer at hand. Steffens might have been the first American groupie when it came to pleading for various causes.

I wish that *The Autobiography of Lincoln Steffens* were still read in this country's high schools, as it was when I was a high school student some forty years ago. It is certainly closer in spirit to both the sins and the possibilities that beset our America than either the whining of Henry Adams or the purposeful eighteenth-century simplicity of Benjamin Franklin. But attractive as Steffens is and interesting as his autobiography continues to be, his was a voice ultimately betrayed not by the writer's insistence on an "I" with which to rival God but by history. An autobiography that seemed to Max Eastman, writing in 1931, "almost a textbook of revolution" today seems portentous and even silly in its political judgments and disingenuous in its personal naiveté. Through what his biographer Justin Kaplan called "the fictive medium of autobiography," Steffens could entertain his readers with some first-rate portraits and some excellent political gossip. His autobiography is a curiously nineteenth-century book about the twentieth century, a freewheeling, self-mythicizing work by a man so intent on being the voice of his times that he can move from a portrait of the young Ernest Hemingway shadowboxing in the streets of Paris to a portrait of his "divine dictator" bombastically tweaking the collective nose of the Rome press corps.

"Consciously and unconsciously," writes Kaplan, "Steffens re-created himself in his own image." This is precisely what the autobiographical voice should allow the writer to do. Unfortunately for Steffens, Eliot knew what he was talking about when he wrote that history was filled with "many cunning corridors." Steffens was ultimately betrayed by history, not by voice. In 1931, his heroic portrait of Mussolini could not yet have become embarrassing because of the Italian invasion of Ethiopia or because of Il Duce's ignominious end. Steffens's worship of the future that worked, called the Soviet Union, was still possible to excuse in 1931. As a journalist who had been plying his trade for half a century, Steffens could assume an edge on the audience for whom he wrote: In 1931 his life invested him with the kind of presence that gave importance to everything he wrote.

The public record is quixotic even when it does not turn out to be openly treacherous. Unless Orwell's nightmare truly is our future and history can be rewritten daily, the public record will continue to betray the writer's voice. Kurt Waldheim's argument is with history. Moses, on the other hand, argues with God. And as demanding as God can be, he at least permits the writer to argue with him—even if the argument can be carried out only under one's breath.

A writer who discusses the autobiographical voice sooner or later is going to have to examine its use in his own work. I wish I were able to do that as someone whose fame and reputation were substantial enough that he might anticipate being misunderstood. Few things please writers more than the opportunity to echo Prufrock's unknown lady and say, "That is not what I meant at all." And how I would welcome the opportunity to criticize Hollywood for having subverted the integrity of my voice with a film—especially if that same Hollywood had made me rich enough through its seductions that I could afford to criticize it. Even those of us who may cast a cold eye on the prospect of being a celebrity with our ten or fifteen minutes in Andy Warhol's sun suspect that we would, if the opportunity arose, enjoy the rewards of celebrity. One may not particularly like caviar, but one would still, I take it, like the opportunity to spread it on his own cracker.

Unfortunately for me, I find myself both primarily an autobiographical writer and a writer whose books do not sell. And that is a peculiar fate. It is one thing to write, say, romantic novels that do not sell or detective stories that do not sell. Such failures do not challenge the self. But my truth is that I still find myself, at the age of fifty-five, wrestling with a life that has been charged and recharged by my imagination with a significance that only hints at ultimate reconciliations. My truth is that, like Franklin, I want my life to serve as exemplum. Like Adams, I want writing about my life to be an act of vengeance upon a universe unaware of that life's very existence. And, like Steffens, I want to yank the child in me up by his toes and see whether I can truly learn to "unlearn all my learning." An autobiographical voice in a writer constitutes no more, and no less, than an attempt to thrust the self against its times.

All the contradictions a man learns to live with are unreconciled in the writer's imagination. Like an awkward, overgrown child, imagination still claims the self, seeks to rework the past. Only the voice of imagination must still battle against the tones that echoed down the same corridors when I was a child. It is still God who cries, "I am" to this writer—and the cry is even louder when one does not, as I do not, believe in God. I tell myself that

God's "I am" creates no sense of obligation in me. But I don't say it aloud. In fact I don't even say it under my breath. After all, that God in whom I do not believe may be listening. In any case I know that imagination will come to my rescue. Sooner or later I will find myself balancing two equally intense memories. In one I am ten years old and have just hit a baseball out of the lot behind the apartment house on Rochambeau Avenue and against the black clock of the liquor store on Bainbridge Avenue. In the other I am a year older and I am lying in bed in a country hospital, my fever-ridden body glued to the sweat-stained sheets, trying to hear the sounds of my own death as a polio virus eats its way through my body. But all I can hear, banging away in my imagination, are the runaway cannons of a past I am already mythicizing. I do not die. And the runaway cannons, it turns out, will bang away forever.

For Henry Adams, that little man I have come to dislike so much, was correct. Unable to say "I am," the autobiographical voice insists on vengeance. It may also insist on other things as it tries to impose structure on the life imposed on the writer. But it certainly insists on vengeance. And the autobiographical writer can avoid rhetoric only by admitting to the source of that rage, by insisting his imagination reorder existence.

Lives are reinvented not with words alone. Proust's madeleine was simply a pastry, but Proust reordered the world through memory of its crumbs. In the last analysis the writer is asked to remain true not to what happened in his life but to the words with which he restructures, reinvents, recreates what happened. Sooner or later even the densest among us learns that using the first-person singular is no guarantee of presence. Any writer can say "I," but "I am" is another matter entirely. Unfortunately, it remains the ability to say "I am" that sets us mumbling to ourselves about how even language cheats us, how it denies us that absolute sense of self, that godly presence, which the voice from within the burning bush hurls at Moses. And so there we are, standing barefoot on the consecrated ground, resentful of that voice from the flames—and even more resentful of the voice we can offer as our own.

In Kafka's house

Like nightmares, private terrors bind themselves to our sense of the possible. The imagination's violence is inflicted by the mind upon itself. And when that violence is made visible, we stand in dread as terror is transformed into reality.

Ever since I took sick with polio at the age of eleven, I have been terrified of waking up one morning to discover I am once again helpless. I am not talking about the prospect of stroke or heart attack or cancer. No matter how life-threatening, ordinary illness is simply among the risks one takes by having been born and growing older. I am talking about my nightmare of enforced isolation, in which I am held captive by the ability of others to structure the aftereffects of my disease.

One can be imprisoned by the world and yet not stand within it. At the heart of my dread I see a human being begging for the space he occupies and the air he breathes. The vision consumes me, even as fantasy. I cannot rid myself of the belief that a person has the right to hold on to the self he has created.

My idea that I have created a self may simply be another false god I choose to worship. I recognize that. Still, the prospect of being forced to function as others command I function is terrifying. I think I could lie without moving, a sentient vegetable, if only I still believed I could maintain allegiance to my idea of who I was and what I had made of my life. I know, of course, that every man and woman desires a strong sense of the self. But the prospect of discovering that one's capacity for living can be defined by others is particularly haunting to a man who has been conscious of his helplessness at some other point in his life.

A few months ago, my terrified vision of helplessness was reawakened as two old friends, a husband and wife visiting the States from the Netherlands, told me what had recently happened to their oldest son. Their story had the effect of making me tremble, so intense was the rage it called forth.

Let me call him Michael. We are curiously tied together, Michael and I, both of our lives radically altered by a physical handicap. We first met when I was the Fulbright lecturer at the University of Leiden during the academic year 1964–1965. My wife and I and our two-year-old son were frequent visitors at Michael's parents' house. Michael was then a young man who had just turned nineteen, twelve years younger than me. We talked in a Dutch-English patois. Michael was intent not only on what the future held in store for him but on the very visible fact that, like him, I was physically crippled. Having lost the use of my legs, I walked on double long-legged braces and crutches.

Michael's own handicap was considerably more severe. He had been born in the early summer of 1945, soon after the war in Europe came to an end. His mother had been pregnant with him during the terrible final winter of that war, what people old enough to remember in western Holland still call the *Hungerwinter*. Men and women crawled in the fields and ate tulip bulbs to keep from starving. Physicians blamed the inadequate nutrition available to his mother for the overwhelming genetic weakness in Michael's arms and legs.

I had already lived for two full decades with the effects of what my virus had done to me. Diligent exercise had given me considerable strength in my arms and shoulders. I could walk mile after mile on my crutches, the fifteen pounds of leather and steel strapped to my legs no more than a metaphor for my sense of power then. Michael's mobility was extremely limited. He was dependent on his parents and his two younger brothers—both of them strong and athletic—to get around.

In August, 1968, as Russian tanks rolled into Prague, I returned to the Netherlands for a second Fulbright year. By this time I had a second son. Once again we were welcomed by Michael's family, and Michael and I renewed our conversations about life and struggle. I wasn't surprised when, a year later, soon after our return to New York, a letter from Michael announced his imminent marriage. Michael wanted me to know that my example had given him hope. He was ready to lead a "normal" life.

I am not a modest man, and I take a great deal of pride in what I have been able to make of my life despite formidable obstacles. But I never wanted to serve as anyone's model of how to live with a severe physical handicap. Looking back, however, it almost seems inevitable that I became a model for Michael. His mother had translated my first book, an account of my encounter with the polio virus, into Dutch. And when he and I talked, Michael would speak quite openly about his feelings, his thoughts, his fears and ambitions, his crippled state. Just before we left Holland in June, 1969, I learned that he had decided to study for the ministry. He had chosen to be "normal." With God's help, he now wrote, he would taste the sacrament of marriage.

A skeptic, I was more suspicious of God's help than was Michael. But in the letter I wrote back, I spoke of how splendidly he had come through, by which I meant not that he had "overcome his handicap" but that he had absorbed the pain of the cripple into his strength as a man. Michael understood what it had taken me years to learn—that a cripple validates his life by creating a sense of his selfhood out of physical pain and chaos. Of course, Michael was a Christian, and for a Christian, suffering binds one to God. But Michael also understood that it was his suffering that gave him the right to choose survival. A nonbeliever could only envy his capacity for faith. From my painfully secular position, the cripple's presence merely testified to a calculus of accident. One could accept the implications of such mathematics, since one's acceptance was beside the point. Both believers and nonbelievers were powerless to change the way things were.

Over the next ten years, I corresponded with Michael's parents. And I heard news of Michael as I heard news of their other children. Once a Christmas card from Michael himself arrived. He offered his warmest wishes on the back of a photograph showing him sitting in an oversized armchair, misshapen legs jutting out from under him, surrounded by wife and two small children. All are smiling.

Michael's father wrote to tell me that his son was minister of a small congregation in the northeastern Netherlands. Although he was, like me, a nonbeliever, with a "normal" father's pride he noted that Michael's sermons were more literate than his small-town congregation could know. He took pleasure, as I took pleasure, in the knowledge that Michael was getting on in the world.

In 1981, when I was again living in Europe, I visited Michael's parents in the small town on the Côte d'Or where they now had a summer home. Michael, I learned, had separated from his wife. But his parents believed that they might yet reconcile their differences. And Michael and his wife did reconcile. But I lost touch with his parents until this past February, when they wrote that they were coming to America for a few weeks. In April they spent three days with us in New York. And it was then that I heard the story that rekindled the primary terror of my imagination—the threat of helpless isolation imposed by someone one loves.

As I listened to Michael's parents, I felt anger, then rage. And then I felt something stronger than anger or rage, a naked, throbbing fear that came from somewhere so deep inside me that it threatened sanity. Pathologies are bred in the bone, conditioned by past expectations. In literature, as Susan Sontag reminded us in *Illness as Metaphor*, illness is usually inappropriate as an image. In life, however, it can be a most appropriate definition—one that thrusts a cripple against his weakness and his strength.

Envision the scene as I envision it. Michael is now a man of forty-four, father of two grown sons, minister of the gospel. He is a respected member of the community. But his life has been defined, as it will continue to be defined, by the nutrients his mother was deprived of during the *Hungerwinter*. The war in Europe made Michael a minor irony in a world filled with irony and horror enough for all tastes. For what was Michael in the Europe of 1945? He had been conceived as Anne Frank and millions of her fellow Jews were murdered, their crime the stigma of having been born; and he sucked for the scarce nutrients that would nourish him into life as death rained ceaselessly across the skies of Europe. Heraclitus had said it thousands of years earlier: Death was everywhere, in the voices of all men. No one who survived, even survived as Michael had survived, had a right to complain.

I close my eyes and watch the scene: a woman pushing a man in a wheelchair into a small room. She takes him from the chair, forces him to the mattress on the floor. Then she takes his crutches and his wheelchair from the room, locks the door. He is to be taught a lesson by his wife-jailer. Other than the mattress on the floor and a straw-seat chair that seems to have been lifted from a Van Gogh painting and placed in the corner of the room, there is no furniture. There is no bathroom. There is no washstand.

He hears his sons, now young men of fifteen and seventeen, move through the house. His sons ignore the closed door. Beyond it lies not their father but a thing defined by their mother. Solitude is misshapen. He may talk like a man. But his sons know that a man—even a minister of the gospel—is not merely speech. A man is body, defining himself by the demands he makes upon the world. Michael demands nothing. Like Kafka's hunger artist, he finds himself more and more attracted to the aesthetics of starvation while he lies on the floor. His world has been turned inside out. His children are his guards, his wife is his jailer, his passion is now to romance his captivity.

I remain purposely calm as I listen. I envision Michael lying inside the locked room, in his own dirt, measuring time in the mind's eyes. No television set, no books, no radio, no newspaper. He can listen to the sounds of his oldest son's guitar. The sound of the guitar soothes, makes him feel part of his family again. He smiles, as if he were once more surrounded by wife and sons, posing for a picture on a Christmas card. He closes his eyes. In memory, he recites verses from the Bible. In imagination, he preaches passionate sermons to congregations hanging breathlessly on his every word.

But if he is God's voice, he can speak in imagination alone. For five days, punctually at three, his wife-jailer unlocks the door and shoves a tray into the room. Focusing his eyes on the tray, he forces his face to remain expressionless. His wife grimaces her displeasure at the sight of Michael on the floor, dissatisfied with what she has created. His solitary kingdom is defined anew by the glass of water, the bread, and the cheese on the tray. He does not crawl to the tray until she has closed and relocked the door. Reduced in size, he crawls to the tray. Michael eats.

His voice survives. It survives five days of hearing itself in the mind alone. It assumes the scale imagination demands. Isaiah, Ezekiel, lamenting with Jeremiah. Never before had Michael felt comfortable with the Book of Ecclesiastes. It was always too Greek, too lacking in Christian hope. But now, in his enforced isolation, he transforms the Preacher word by word. Endurance is a form of love. And as he lies alone on the mattress in the empty room, Michael is determined to endure. If he can outlast captivity, he will, he knows, again become human.

He hears wife and sons speaking with considerable agitation in the vestibule. He hears the front door slam. Silence descends on the house. Too weak simply to crawl, Michael twists and slithers to the door. He is not the serpent in the Garden. This is his house, not Eden. He reaches up to touch the lock and the door springs free. They have deliberately left it open. He moves to the entrance of the house, slithering to the front door. It, too, is unlocked. A neighbor spies him as he twists outside, slithering like a commando moving beneath barbed wire. Amazement on his face, the neighbor hesitantly approaches. Michael is covered with dirt. There is blood on his forehead where he scraped it against the doorjamb. He smells of feces and dried urine and sweat and stale days and nights. The neighbor reaches down, touches him, furtively, as if Michael were some jellylike blob in a low-budget horror film. Michael smiles. The neighbor will telephone the police. No, Michael insists, better if he simply helps him get into his car.

He slithers to the car. With the neighbor cradling him in a fireman's lift, he gets inside. As he suspected, the door of the car has been left open. The keys wait in the ignition. Michael feels lightheaded—from hunger, from his own smell, from the unexpected gift of freedom, from the outrage and distaste so visible on his neighbor's face. Michael turns the key, touches the specially constructed hand controls, smiles his gratitude at the neighbor, who angrily slams the car door shut. Michael drives off, no longer a captive. He has been tested.

And he has been sentenced. To helplessness. But he remains a believer. "People like us," I remember him saying as he told me of his decision to enter the ministry, "have been chosen to suffer for the rest of mankind. With our lives, God demonstrates his love for the world." I remember how I resisted the temptation to make some caustic comment about God's love. Instead, I told him that I believed people chose their fates from what was available to them at the time of their choosing. Michael was adamant. God, he insisted, had chosen him. And whether I knew it or not, he had chosen me, too. If so, I remember thinking at the time, his God was capricious enough to serve as ringmaster for this century's circus. But I didn't say anything. Michael was determined to survive. His faith was the price he paid for that survival.

Michael drove to the house of a parishioner, a woman his wife insisted he was sleeping with. He saw her only for work related to church projects. Better, I thought, if they had been sleeping together. To be imprisoned for a crime committed—however ludicrous that "crime" may be—would have lent structure to Michael's ordeal. One can be grateful even for structure.

The woman bathes him, washing away the smell of captivity. She sets the table, listens to Michael say grace. Like the neighbor, she wants to call the police. Michael refuses. She must understand. He is a minister. He is a cripple. He is a burden. To himself and to others. There will be no calls to the police. In another's house, Michael sleeps. A proper sleep in a proper bed. Without knowing it, he has read Kafka up close.

Thinking about that story makes me want to howl like a wounded animal, to stick my hand through glass. Thinking about that story makes me believe that only in the breaking does life make sense.

I am fifty-five years old. I have created a life, built it piece by piece. And I can be thrust aside, locked away, made susceptible to the same terror as Michael. I shiver as I envision myself in Michael's place. Reeking of humiliation, imprisoned by those one loves, tested by a calculating malevolence. Michael told himself he was being tested by his God. The test is as absurd as the genetics created by the *Hungerwinter*. Accidents should not be tragic but comic—Chaplin falling through an open manhole.

I feel my sanity threatened because Michael's nightmare is also my own. Michael's fate was to become the self reduced to its scars. We are, Michael and I, creations of Susan Sontag's "more onerous citizenship." It is not a citizenship one chooses. But endemic to the life one claims from the skewered ambitions and twisted dreams of one's actual life are the choices one makes. Citizens act, think, create. In his own eyes, Michael has been singled out by his God. His problem is to prove himself worthy of having been singled out. Mine is to continue to earn a self through the everyday rigors of living with disease.

In the struggle between sickness and health, the forces of light and the forces of darkness, Michael and I are simply soldiers in the ranks. Thomas Mann pits Hans Castorp and his cousin Joachim against one another in his great novel *The Magic Mountain*. Hans is indolent in his willingness to allow disease to define his life; Joachim refuses to give in to what disease has made of him. Mann, always the master ironist, destroys Joachim because he insists on denying the defining power of disease.

What infuriates me is not the vision of Michael lying in his own filth on a bare mattress in a bare room. What infuriates me is that the genetics that defined him made him so dependent on others that his capacity to claim a self could be stolen by a bitter wife and fearful sons. To be defined as what feminists like to call an "object," a thing whose existence can be made over by others, is nightmarish. And yet, there was a time when Michael was loved, when his sons sang to him, when his wife rested her head on his childishly weak arms, seeking to unlock the self she was ultimately to lock away.

Think of Michael lying in that room. He longs for companionship, hears voices, preaches to thousands in his mind, transforms himself—like the early Christian martyrs—into a man deemed worthy of the God who has so capriciously robbed him of physical presence. Think of Michael dismissing all theories of probability, because, like Kafka, he has come to realize that whatever happened was somehow deserved. Think of Michael opening himself up to the fears of others, grafting them onto his own life.

Memory blesses terror. When I was thirteen and returned to my neighborhood from two years in an upstate hospital, my mother, I remember, walked into the apartment one September afternoon, face tear-streaked and ashen. The butcher's wife had just told her that my illness was God's judgment—*on her*. The butcher's wife was known throughout the neighborhood as "not right in the head," a knowledge that should have made it easy to dismiss what she said. Sitting in the sawdust-strewn butcher shop, childless, she would knit, our own Madame de Farge, mumbling incantations in Yiddish to placate a god of vengeance and to impose order on an evil, crazed universe. Her eyes would blank out the world, or else they would sparkle with the electric blue-and-green current of the mad.

Mad or sane, the butcher's wife had touched my mother's center, as Kafka touches our centers. For she had voiced precisely what my mother herself believed about disease in her own fear-ravaged heart. Illness was judgment. The slings and arrows of fortune might be outrageous; they were never undeserved. Accident, illness, war, famine, disease: punishments visited upon one by the master of the universe.

To call this superstition is useless. For the butcher's wife and my mother simply believed what far more sophisticated and rational people believe even today about disease: It is judgment rendered. Through illness, justice can be meted out. The victim of accident turns out not to be a victim by accident. It is not the meaning of illness that is beyond understanding. The meaning can easily be understood. For to dwell in Kafka's House is to discover that judgment dwells alongside one. And to be a "victim of disease" is to be tested, tried, made better, punished, reborn.

Anyone who has dealt with a long-term illness or accident soon recognizes the extent to which his or her own view of it is judgmental. In Kafka's House, a sense of mystery does not eliminate cause and effect. One loses one's body to disease, but one also loses it to memory. And it becomes increasingly difficult, as one focuses on that loss, not to read into it some greater significance than it merits. Writer and physician and theologian join hands in assigning responsibility. Disease has somehow been welcomed, accident has somehow been sought out. Psychosomatic illness may not be as fashionable an intellectual theory today as it was twenty years ago. But we continue to speak of disease-welcoming personalities and accident-embracing tendencies. A modern vocabulary makes "scientific" the fears and superstitions operating on both the butcher's mad wife and my own judgment-obsessed mother.

Did Michael, as a believer, view his treatment at the hands of his jailer-wife and guard-sons as another trial, a further test to be endured? Pain cannot be allowed to be fortuitous. Michael and his wife and sons were actors together in some metaphysical drama. In some corner of his mind, Michael achieved purgation. He had suffered, he had endured—and his suffering and endurance were meaningful. They proved him worthy.

Does Michael continue to view the body isolated from its fellow humans, assigned a place in the prison of another's making, as fit punishment for the sin of having been born with genetic defects? As he sleeps now alongside his new wife—yes, the parishioner who cleansed him—does he remember that disease, too, is a sharing, a communion of sorts? Does he recognize how it inflicts itself on others? Does he see how it spurs the imagination—Kafka's aphorisms, Poe's visions, Modigliani wandering through the night-bound streets of Europe? Incapacity can be made into a fiery judgment on the world.

How does time pass in the solitary anguish Michael experienced? Picture an insect following its antennae across wall after wall. A wall is a surface and a surface must be crawled across—up and down, right and left, circle and square, movement following movement.

When Michael first told me he had decided on the ministry, I asked him whether he had read Kafka. He hadn't. I hope he never does. Let him conceive of himself as an original. Let him think of his suffering as a reification of the self. Even the movement of an insect possesses boundaries when contained within the mind. On the blank page, Kafka stands more powerful than the father he created from memory's space. To the tubercular writer, Gregor Samsa embodies the ordinary drabness of suffering. A tedious process, illness, breeding not despair and angst but the singular determination to get through one's days and nights. Learning to live with disease is intimate, even seductive. The parts of Michael's body miraculously change themselves into animated sensors testing the world the way a blind man tests the pitch and dip of a street with his cane.

Illness can be a metaphor only to those determined to remain ignorant of its truth. Susan Sontag was certainly correct in that. And by the same token, illness can be therapeutic only to those determined to avoid its tedium. It is not a process by which one offers the self for assessment. But it is a state of being in which one can uncover the self, stand it naked and clear before the imagination. Has Michael learned this? He never complained, but as a believer he could never accept the sheer diceyness of what had happened to him. He accepts the responsibility of resisting the consequences of his birth, for he senses that such resistance affirms what is most human in him. But he cannot resist the temptation to make illness even more significant than it is. The truth is that the only thing he should be concerned with is not the ideology one reads into disease but the terms by which one establishes resistance to its effects. I wonder whether Michael ever learned that he cannot cure himself by endowing suffering with the theological equivalent of the Good Housekeeping Seal of Approval.

Individuals do not succumb to cancer or to heart attacks because they want to succumb. They are simply "struck down," an arbitrary striking that makes no sense and needs no justification. True, we now know that certain individuals possess a genetic susceptibility to specific diseases and conditions. But these are gambler's odds, shaped by gambler's recognitions. In selecting victims, disease and accident are fortuitous and illogical. Michael was born with weakened limbs because his mother was pregnant during a time of human-caused famine. Judgment was rendered here not by God but by man. Michael was the victim of the same political history that created the Holocaust and left the cities of Europe in rubble.

The mathematical probability of illness or accident can be created by any number of possible factors. For Michael, the war. For me, a prospectively innocent two weeks at summer camp. A reminder for all philosophers of chance. On the bus going to camp, we were seated according to height. I was a tall boy, taller than the two friends from the neighborhood I was going to camp with. I was made to sit next to another, taller boy. His name was Jerry, he had watery blue eyes, and by the time we arrived at the camp I had invited him to share a bunk with me and my two friends from the neighborhood. Eleven days later Jerry and I were in a small country hospital fighting to stay alive. Jerry died. I lost the use of my legs to the virus. My two friends returned to the city untouched. Was it simply a time when a capricious God or a quixotic fate had it in for taller boys? Would shorter boys have their turn next year? Did Jerry and I share an "inclination" to embrace the disease-carrying virus? Were my two neighborhood friends better prepared to resist its siren song? A simple cast of the dice is never enough: Judgment demands more magical incantations.

Think of what our age has created from such spiritual voodoo. In the name of diagnosis, the mind has been burdened with the task of saving us from illness. "Canst thou administer to a mind diseased?" cries Macbeth. In our time, he would subscribe to a journal of holistic medicine. Think healthy and you are healthy. The intensity of our interest in quackery staggers the rational mind. We peddle cures for virtually every condition known to man: cancer, acne, heart attack, impotence, stroke, hair loss, pneumonia, bad breath. We are deluged by books urging us to eat our way to health, to will our way to health, to exercise our way to health, to fuck our way to health. Physicians vie with one another for the chance to treat the soul rather than the body—or, better yet, to treat the body through treating the soul. *Amor vincit omnia!*

And we veteran denizens of Kafka's House, even we are absorbed not by the pathology of disease but by the psychology of those who "allowed" disease to enter their lives. How curious that it is Michael, not his wife, whose motives I probe. The bearer of the virus is of little interest; the victim commands our attention. In Kafka's House, one learns to view not the terrorized but terror with compassion. Just as in certain writings about the Holocaust the implicit question addressed to the Jews is, "How could *you* let this happen?" so Michael discovers he has been condemned to answer his wife-jailer and guard-sons as they cry out, "How could *you* allow us to do this?"

Ours is a century which views weakness as sin. Even those whose lives are intertwined with the lives of the weak become victims of their victimization. "Why me?" compels "Why them?" The victims of the victim become the significant bearers of his pain. His scars—the useless legs, the weak arms, the bent shoulders—are their burden. The mind of the jailer haunts the prisoner. Michael's true shame is for what he has done to those who once loved him.

It has been almost three years since Michael's sons last spoke to their father. Curiously, I can understand that. They lack the intensity of his obsession. And they lack his belief, his sense of having been selected to suffer for the rest of humanity. We do not live inside a Malamud novel. They *are* the rest of humanity. Kafka's father is the father they desire, created as need dictates. To ask them to love their father is to ask them to deny themselves. His ravaged body will forever rebuke their need for strength.

What makes their resentment understandable is that they feel trapped. Disease truly is a sharing. But its burdens and rewards are unequal. Think of Michael's two sons, men themselves now, aware from the time they were toddlers that they were physically more powerful than the man they called father. A father who is God's solitary beggar rebukes the very power they seek. What they desire is a father against whom revolt might be conventional, a father who seems powerful and overwhelming, a father like Kafka's father. What they have gotten is a father who inspires in them rage intense enough to create its own metaphysics of injustice. To assert the self, they need to pull down what is strong. A father lacking power is a father who demands not revolt but compassion. Michael's presence offends their need. His smile, his piety, his endurance all conspire to indict his sons, to deny their urgent need to test the world for themselves.

And even as I rage at her, I try to see that bare room through the eyes of Michael's jailer, his wife. Do I condemn her inability to live with her husband's bargains with God? Was locking Michael in that room her confession of failure? The idea is as soothing as it is obscene, as if Michael had to be imprisoned and humiliated, left in the dirt and smells of his affliction, so that his wife could see herself as something other than servant to his needs. Did she, I wonder, share Michael's sense that Christians are repositories of suffering? That their burden is the world's salvation? The lame, the halt, the blind: Was her anger at Michael fueled when he took the burden of being human from her heart and mind?

Despite Sontag's splendid effort, writers will continue to use illness as metaphor. Disease so easily springs out of control. And what better language for condemnation, for evil, for receiving one's just and unjust reward or punishment? Cancer, heart attack, AIDS, and diseases yet to be discovered—a stream of metaphors, all promising retribution against hedonism and excess. The body's unconscious revenge upon the depths of depravity available to the modern body.

And since we are creatures of paradox, we will employ the metaphors even while we continue to live in a culture that obligates man to be "healthy," a culture in which all disease can be withstood, conquered through the exertion of the individual will.

The surgeon specializing in the removal of cancerous tumors becomes a Doctor of Love specializing in the removal of moribund fears of death and dying. From a magazine cover his face stares up at me. Scalp shaved naked to the wind, eyes burning with the power and truth of his message, this is not the butcher's mad wife, finger pointing *J'accuse* at my guilt-ridden mother. Still, I cannot help wondering what the Doctor of Love would say to Michael? Or to Michael's sons? Or to Michael's ex-wife? Would he offer the power of positive thinking? New sons? New wives? New beliefs? Stabbed by reality, Michael yet hungers after salvation. He, too, searches for cause and effect. In this he is no different from the Doctor of Love.

For what did Michael want? That his faith be tested?

And the doors shall be shut in the streets,
When the sound of the grinding is low.

Well, the door was shut. But after forty-four years of living as a cripple, Michael takes the longer view. Like the Doctor of Love, he will define each stage of his life, each approaching cataclysm. The humiliated body is a mere extension of pain. Michael still believes. He still hungers after inner light. He remains an accountant of the soul, demanding spiritual compensation for a useless body.

It is a grinding obscenity, this need to authenticate suffering. Michael has become a co-conspirator in his victimization. Perhaps the Doctor of Love is really convinced that Michael has power over his own suffering. Perhaps he can convince Michael of the truth of what Michael already believes, that suffering itself is merely symptomatic of some breakdown in one's spiritual balance. I know better. Disease is indeed personal. And what we make of it a reflection of need. But truth is equally personal. Michael was not responsible for the barbarism that led to the *Hungerwinter* of 1944–1945 and I was not responsible for the chance encounter that allowed the virus to slip into my bloodstream in the summer of 1944. Punishment has nothing to do with the crime—unless the crime is defined as merely being human.

And perhaps it should be. To be "struck down" is a most human victimization. Given the keys to Kafka's House, one approaches prospective tenancy there prepared to confront the question of what made one's residence possible. "The romantic idea that the disease expresses the character," Sontag writes, "is invariably extended to assert that the character causes the disease—because it has not expressed itself." Even for Kafka, the voice of tuberculosis demanded that he reject disease and assert his longing for health. How he envied the self-confident and "normal," those who had neither the time nor the patience required by disease. To claim power is also to claim health.

And the man who is "successful" at creating a life out of the aftereffects of disease—as, however immodest it is to write, I have been—discovers that he must, sooner or later, fight against an inflated notion of what it is he has achieved. When a mutual friend praised Franz Rozenzweig's courage in living with the pain and suffering inflicted on him by a long struggle with cancer, Freud, doomed to undergo the same long struggle, is reported to have said, "What else can he do?" Freud understood that the real question each of us must answer is no different from the question "normal" men and women face: What are the terms with which one lives with disease?

For the man or woman who has successfully "rehabilitated" the self (how awkward the vocabulary of disease, as if language were intended to keep abstract what is so intimate and personal) feels the temptation to make disease self-referential. The primacy of the self does not come from the bargains we strike with our terror: It can just as easily emerge out of what disease has wrought, out of "overcoming" disease. The man who competes in a wheelchair marathon does not view his effort as a mockery of form but as a way of turning stigma upon itself. Having "come through," having "overcome his handicap," he invests what he has done with a morality of its own. "I came, I saw, I conquered!" can so easily be transformed into "I suffered, I overcame, I endured!" It is not, finally, the life one seeks to redeem—it is the disease. For it is the disease that challenges the self to be "better" than it was.

Hans Castorp discovers that, if he is to be made conscious, he must affirm the power of disease that has snatched him from the jaws of health. In seeking shelter in Kafka's House, he deserts the humdrum and banal for the possibility of the erotic and exciting. Made physically smaller, the self suddenly looms larger. To be doomed by illness is to learn how to refuse the temptation of the ordinary and settled. Were I given to looking for signs, I would point out that as they came to the ends of their lives, Kafka and Hemingway switched roles—the one insisting on the need to "overcome" disease and accept the healthy, the other sticking a shotgun in his mouth to blow his "healthy" head away.

I am fifteen minutes early. I park across the street from the restaurant where my friend Ted and I are to meet for dinner. It is no more than thirty feet from where I have parked to the door. A year ago, when Ted and I last met for dinner, I walked into the restaurant on my crutches, as I had been doing for forty years. But walking has become increasingly difficult, and my mind keeps flashing on the wheelchair folded in the trunk of my car.

The question is not trivial. Ted has never seen me in a wheelchair. He has known me for thirty years as the man who has "overcome" the virus through the power of his will (*and* the crutches beneath his shoulders, *and* the braces strapped to his legs). It is how he first knew me, when we met as graduate students at Columbia. And now he has joined me in Kafka's House, each of us singular in illness. Curiously touched by shame, I reach for the crutches and carefully walk into the restaurant.

Ted arrives after I am seated at the table. He looks as he looked thirty years ago. Only he moves slowly, with trepidation, carefully placing one foot in front of the other, like a drunk trying to convince friends he has control and forcing a caution that runs against the grain of his temperament. He spots me, smiles, threads his way between tables across the nubbed industrial carpeting as if some potent unmarked danger were twisted into its fibers waiting to trip him up. "Every step I take," he said to me over the telephone, "makes me feel as if I'm about to be hit. Rheumatoid arthritis. It's a second babyhood." And then, laughing, "And no prospect of growing out of this one."

He sits down across from me, knees bending slowly, like an uncoordinated girl in the third grade preparing for her turn at jump-rope. My friend Ted is afraid—and what he is afraid of, I suspect, is this sudden residence in Kafka's House, where even at dinner with an old friend, himself a resident there, he must stand alone.

Like death, disease is a personal discovery. "It's more curious than bad," he says, anticipating the question I want to ask. "I invent new ways for everything. I never thought about whether or not I was strong enough. I never had to. Now I'm always trying to outwit circumstance."

The smallest action takes on a new magnitude when one must pitch his tent in disease. It is not the halting steps of the cripple he has become that disturbs Ted. Nor even the knowledge that he will stretch memory for the Little All-American halfback he once was. Already forgotten is the party three years ago, to celebrate the ability of a man turned fifty to impose his physical presence on a birthday gathering intended to deny time's passing. No one appreciates better than my friend Ted the irony that transforms a man who loved the physical self even more than he loved Joyce's prose or John Huston's films. In Kafka's House, I remind myself, all are welcome. But the newly invited are uncomfortable, nervous, afraid to make themselves at home. One moves quickly in being forced to move slowly. Condemned now to wait for a porter to carry his bags at an airport or train station, Ted's mind hungers for its own past. At what point will it be not his luggage but himself that must be carried?

No matter how broken, my friend Ted still possesses the memory of the body he once assumed would always remain dependable, growing older into grace but not into disease. He had trusted that body more than he could possibly trust another human being. But he can accept the irony of being betrayed by that in which he had invested so much. He is a literary man, and he knew about Kafka's House long before it was decided he must live there.

As graduate students we used to meet in another restaurant. We would nurse beers after class, discussing the writers we were determined to emulate and the novels we wanted to write, arguing the world back and forth, as only the young who want to be writers can argue, circling ambition's shadow like boxers searching for an opening. Exhilarating arguments, exhausting because neither of us could bend beneath the weight of carrying the record. In such a world, health was assumed. There was no room for illness. Not when the world offered itself to be cracked apart like a walnut.

Only I was a mere eleven years beyond the confrontation with the virus that had left me without the use of my legs. I *knew* the dictates of disease. "Get the crutches," I say as we prepare to leave. Ted had placed my crutches behind the bar because the booth in which we sat was narrow. Ted stares at me, puzzled. "The crutches," I repeat. "You put them behind the bar."

Ted shakes his head. "I always have to remind myself you need them," he says. "I forget."

I had lived in Kafka's House for more than a decade by then. And I knew I was destined to live there for the rest of my life. That was years before I met Michael, three decades before I watched this same friend, painfully crippled himself, slip past the surety of his body into the sour comings and goings of learning to live with disease. I was still intent on "overcoming" back then, and I was as willing to accept my friend Ted's flattery as I was to make a weapon of incapacity. Perhaps that was what I had learned from the years I had already spent in Kafka's House—that while I could not will my way to health I nonetheless could create a tone for my presence out of what the virus had left. If a mind so finely tuned as Kafka's could succumb to the desire to be "normal," then perhaps I could be excused for condemning myself to project the image I was so determined to project. To tell me I had "overcome a handicap" was to affirm the self I had worked so hard to create.

Had I continued to believe I had "overcome" what would always dominate my existence, I would have been trapped in delusion. There are moments when one forgets that no one lives by choice in Kafka's House. But residence there had prepared me for the fear and bewilderment I would see in the face of my friend Ted. And residence there made unforgettable the terror of someday finding myself helpless, bound to the obligations of others as I twist and squirm in my mind. To endure is not enough. I know that, now that I have lived long enough in Kafka's House to understand that the past expects the future. Maybe what I should have said to my friend Ted, as we sat in that Greenwich Village restaurant, was that just as my terror had been Michael's nightmare, so his nightmare was already my past. For he had come to visit in Kafka's House, only to find that, like Hans Castorp on his mountain, he had earned a proper residence there.

Design by David Bullen
Typeset in Mergenthaler Berkeley Olde Style
by Wilsted & Taylor
Printed by Maple-Vail
on acid-free paper